THE LONDON MARKET GUIDE

Written by Andrew Kershman
Production: Susi Koch & Andrew Kershman.
Design & Maps: Susi Koch.
Photography: Susi Koch & Andrew Kershman.
Illustrations: Sebastian Airey.
Editors: Jenny Lacey, Brynmor Lloyd-Evans & Henry Cook.
With special thanks to: NKN, Artec, Andy Sievewright, Louise Miller & Andrea Davidson.
With help from the **Prince's Youth Business Trust.**

First Published in 1994 by
METRO PUBLICATIONS
PO BOX 6336
LONDON
N1 6PY

Printed in Great Britain By:
The Burlington Press
Foxton
Cambridge

© Metro Publications
1994 (1st edition)
ISBN 0 9522914 0 1

CONTENTS

INTRODUCTION

With the rise of the superstore and the expansion of chain stores, shopping is becoming an increasingly predictable past time. Street markets are one of the last avenues of escape from this dreary trend, and nowhere is more famed for its street markets than London. Brandishing a well thumbed copy of this book you should be able to explore them with confidence.

In writing this book I've tried to keep you, the gentle reader, in mind. The chances are you're either one of the 16 million visitors to London wanting to see a little bit more of the capital and it's people, or one of those 7 million Londoners in search of bargains and the occasional day out. You might even be interested in trading from one of the markets mentioned. To help you find out where a particular market is there's a map showing all the markets with an index. The big markets have detailed maps so that you don't miss anything. At the back of the book a table shows which markets are open on which days. There's also a subject index to help you find what you're looking for, and a tube map to help you get there. In addition, The London Market Guide is the first publication to give you all the contact details if you're interested in getting a stall.

I've avoided just giving the positive side of the markets. If a market is expensive, congested or unfriendly I've said so. I hope no one will be too offended by what has been written. The intention has been to encourage people to visit London's markets. I've found some incredible bargains and had a great time in the course of researching this book. I hope you have some fun using it. The most important piece of advice I can give you is to look at the people as well as the things they sell. It's the people, shouting, talking, eating and laughing that make the markets of London worth visiting.

Andrew Kershman
Hackney 1994

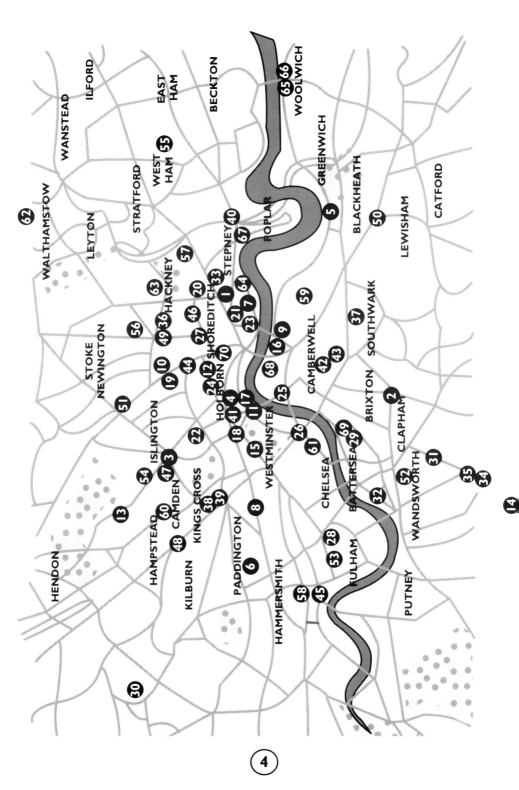

ICON INDEX

 antiques

 music (records tapes. CD's)

 books

 towels bedding

 fresh meat

 shoes

 fruit & veg

 haberdashery

 pubs

 furniture

 produce

 kitchenware household goods

 cloth

 fresh fish

 pet supplies

 clothing

 cut flowers & plants

 toys

 fresh coffee

 hardware

 toiletries

 cafes & restaurants

 bric-a-brac

 fresh bread

Brick Lane
Brixton
Camden
Covent Garden
Greenwich
Portobello Road
Petticoat Lane

BiG MARKETS

INTRODUCTION

Is big best? Does size matter when it comes to consumer satisfaction? The answer is a big YES! All the markets in this chapter are humungus and offer the eager shopper and laid-back potterer hours of entertainment. Each market has it's own appeal so have a read before you go. Camden market is a great day out for the young and trendy, but a nightmare for those whose hormones long ago settled down.

The markets in this chapter are also very varied. Brixton has a good mix of fresh food and second-hand clobber, Greenwich has both old and new clothes as well as furniture, while Portobello has just about everything from antiques to food. Many of the markets are also sited in interesting areas with good shops and cafes to complement what the market offers, they're all shown on the market maps and mentioned in the text.

Having returned home weighed down with goodies, don't restrict yourself to the big mothers; have a look at the specialist, local and wholesale markets, and remember that small can be beautiful...

Brick Lane (north of the railway bridge up to Bethnal Green Road), Cheshire and Sclater Street.
Tube: Liverpool Street (Metro & Circle Lines), Aldgate East (District), Old Street (Northern), Shoreditch (East London Line).
Buses: 8 (Bethnal Green). 5, 22A, 22B, 26, 35, 47, 48, 55, 67, 78, 149, 243, 243A, 505 (Shoreditch High Street).
Open: Sundays 6am-1pm.

Brick Lane Market is not a place for those of a delicate constitution. It's big, dirty, and disorganized. This might not sound like the most wonderful shopping experience, but to those who are prepared to roll up their sleeves and hunt for strange and unusual bargains, this is paradise. The best thing about the market is that it's full of surprises. Amongst all the rubbish, you might just find the trinket, book or item of clothing you've been looking for. On a recent visit I discovered a pair of cream linen trousers for £2.50, this was on a stall selling a mixture of children's clothes and records.

Bethnal Green Road-Sclater Street (Junk, Electrical Goods, Hardware, Toiletries, Bikes & Food)

The corner of Bethnal Green Road and Commercial Street is usually full of strange characters selling just about anything from bikes to records on the pavement. Sclater Street is one of the main arteries of the market, dealing largely in new bikes, toys, DIY equipment and new clothes. The trainers stall on the left hand side is worth a visit - Air Pegasus are only £42. There is a courtyard either side of Sclater Street. To the right can be found second-hand clothes, electrical goods, tools and toiletries. To the left are mainly new stalls dealing in bags, bread, electrical goods and bikes. A permanent fixture of the market is the MelPack lorry selling frozen meat. The MC is brilliant - a sort of cross between John Prescott and Billy Graham. After listening, many lifelong vegetarians have been known to raise their hands for some of his economy sausages.

Brick Lane (Fruit & Veg, New Clothes, Bric-a-Brac)

The northern end of Brick Lane deals mainly in new clothes. The best thing about this part of the market is the bagel bakery at the top. It's from here that most experienced visitors gain sustenance before embarking on their quest.

At the junction of Brick Lane, Sclater and Cheshire Street the fruit and veg pitchers call for their trade, selling large quantities at low prices. Further along, under the railway arches, are indoor lock-ups. If you can stand the damp dungeon-like atmosphere it's worth taking a look. Amid all the old furniture, books, clothes and telephones you might find something special.

1. BEIGEL BAKERY
2. GINA'S RESTAURANT

(a) COURTYARD
(b) COURTYARD
(c) INDOOR MARKET
(d) INDOOR MARKET
(e) INDOOR MARKET

BETHNAL GREEN ROAD

GRANBY ST

CHILTON ST

BACON ST

SCLATER ST

BRICK LANE

CHESHIRE STREET

GRIMSBY ST.

SHOREDITCH

P

Cheshire Street (Clothes, Prints, Cameras and Books)

Despite the closure of the courtyard between Kerbla Street and St Mathew's Row this is still the best part of the market. Most of the new stalls are concentrated at the Brick Lane end of Cheshire Street, selling poor quality clothing at low prices. The street becomes more disorderly further along as the junk stalls come into their own. The poster and print stall is one of the few that manages to mix novelty with order, as does the book shop a little further along. For the rest it's a matter of sorting through the debris to find something of interest. Just after Kerbla Street on the right is an indoor part to the market . Here you can find any-

thing from books and expensive camera equipment to new kitchenware - there's even a stall selling boxing memorabilia. Further along, the small side street called Hare Marsh marks the end of the market with its assortment of old tools and furniture littering the pavement.

Getting a Stall

Contact Tower Hamlets Central Market Office (see Appendix) for a licence and then visit the Bethnal Green Neighbourhood office:
One Stop Shop
10 Turin Street E2
071 739 6339

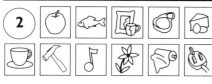

Brixton Station Road, Pope's Road, Atlantic Road, Electric Road & Electric Avenue.
Tube/BR: Brixton (Victoria and Northern Line)
Buses: 3, 3B, 59, 109, 133, 159 (Brixton Road).
35, 45, 45A, P4 (Coldharbour Lane).
2, 322 (Stockwell Road).
Open: Monday-Saturday 8am-5.30pm. Wednesday 8am-1pm.

Until the 1960's Brixton and its market could have been compared to an ageing Edwardian lady, still showing the remnants of a grander past, but facing a pretty dismal future. The West Indian community added something a little bit stronger to the old dame's night cap and since then she hasn't looked back. These days Brixton market is just about the best weekday market south of the river. Within its maze of roads, arcades and railway arches there's fresh food, wonderful African fabrics, bits and pieces for the home and a good mix of second-hand things for the bargain hunter. What's more, Brixton has some great cafes where you can sit and chill if it all proves too much.

Brixton Station Road

The western end of this street (towards Brixton Road) has stalls selling fruit and veg, cut flowers, African objects and a very good hardware shop where you can pick up a 20 piece socket set for only £3.99. If you follow your ears you'll come to Fe Real Muzic where all sorts of soul, rap and reggae are played and sold. Next door the Tacaranda Gardens offers houmous and salad with pitta bread for only £1.95, and serves a pretty mean coffee. Past the junction with Pope's Road there's second-hand clothes and electrical equipment, as well as a good selection of bric-a-brac. If you're prepared to hunt, this is a great place to dig up a bargain.

Pope's Road

This narrow road offers fruit and veg from all over the world. There's also cheap and cheerful new clothing and shoes, jewellery and a stall selling beans and pulses. It's a great place to come on a busy lunch-time to watch punter and pitcher argue over the quality and price of produce before reaching grudging agreement.

Granville Arcade

This is the largest arcade in Brixton with light blue walls and skylights avoiding the gloom of most indoor markets. There's lots of exotic fruit and veg to choose from, unusual fish such as smoked angera at £2.99lb, and colourful Nasseri African fabrics for as little as £7 for 6 yards. There's also a wig shop for the follically impaired.

Reliance Arcade

This arcade is nothing more than a narrow passageway crammed with stalls selling cheap, but not very interesting new clothing. The only thing worth mentioning is the excellent camera shop at the Brixton Road entrance to the arcade.

Market Row

At the entrance to this arcade is a small shop specializing in military ware, which sells DM's and other items at below the usual price. Inside there's a good selection of food stalls and a particularly fine fish stall with things like goat fish and blue runner available. The arcade also has two of the best cafes in Brixton, namely Kafe Pushkar and the Pizzeria and Coffee Bar, both great places to rest after several hours intensive shopping.

1 TACARANDA GARDENS

2 ATLANTIC CAFE

3 CAFE PUSHKAR

4 KIM'S CAFE

5 TERMINUS SNACK BAR

6 PIZZERIA AND COFFEE BAR

7 FE REAL MUZIC

8 COMBINED SERVICES SUPPLY

9 NASSERI FABRICS LTD.

(a) ARCHWAY ARCADE

(b) GRANVILLE ARCADE

(c) MARKET ROW

(d) RELIANCE ARCADE

(e) STATION ARCADE

Electric Avenue

This was one of the first streets to get electricity in the 1880's, hence the name. Like Pope's Road this thoroughfare has all types of fruit and veg, but in addition lots of butchers and grocery shops which complement the market. At the high street end there are more stalls offering clothes, pot plants (potted plants that is) and a good haberdashers.

Getting a Stall

For more details contact:
Brixton Market Office
Baylis Road SE1
071 926 2530 (9-10.30am or 3-4pm).

(3)

Extending the length of Camden High Street, and the southern end of Chalk Farm Road.
Tube: Camden Town, Chalk Farm (Northern).
Buses: 24, 27, 29, 31, 68, 134, 135, 168, 214, 253 274, C2 (Camden High Street).

Since the early 70's the markets in Camden Town - there are at least six - have established a reputation as a sort of Mecca for those in search of street cred. Thousands of disciples come here every weekend seeking the holy chalice of a certain cut of trouser or the latest style of shirt. The stalls are pretty quick to react to a trend, and always have a good stock of basics like leather jackets, T-shirts and 501's. What detracts from the market is the high price of things, and the hostile, sleazy atmosphere of the place.

However, for many teenagers escaping from their poster clad rooms for the weekend, expensive squalor is just what they're looking for. If you want to avoid adolescent hysteria either get here early when they're still tucked up in bed, or try on a Thursday or Friday when the southern part of the market is running on a more subdued level.

CAMDEN MARKET
Camden High Street, south of Buck Street.
Open: Thursday-Sunday 9am-5pm.

If you like being among the throng then visit this place at the weekend when it's packed. For those in search of a more genteel potter around the market, come on a Thursday or Friday, when the atmosphere is generally more relaxed. The clothing on offer is a mixture of old and new; the predictably trendy and the unusual. On one stall a well made rather smooth, ribbed jacket was on offer for £35. At another a good quality zip collar short sleeve top was going for £15, the price fell immediately to £10 without so much as a haggle!

Camden Market is not only a good place to find clothes. There are many stalls selling jewellery, records and tapes, and one offering "psycotropic herbs", "developed from experience in shamanic working", with names like "Old Beastie" and "Dragon Brew", along with water filtered appliances with which to consume them. In this way it is possible both to clothe your body and then have an out of body experience to admire yourself...

Getting a Stall
On Thursday and Friday you should be able to get a stall, just turn up and speak with Peter in his office at the back of the market. Friday and Saturday are something of a closed shop - all the stalls are taken, there's no waiting list, and if a vacancy arises it's filled by one of those in the know - nuff said...

CAMDEN CANAL MARKET

North east of the canal, connecting with Castle Haven Road.
Open: Saturday-Sunday 10am-6pm.

In this cramped warren can be found all manner of collectables, clothes, books and even a stall selling sewing machines. At the far end of the market on the entrance to Castle Haven Street is a stall selling bikes - although none of them can be described as top of the range.

(a) ELECTRIC MARKET

(b) CAMDEN MARKET

(c) CANAL MARKET

(d) CAMDEN LOCK

(e) STABLES MARKET

(f) PEDESTRIAN BRIGDE
(where you queue for stalls)

Getting a Stall

Just turn up by 8.30am and have a chat with Fred. You're more likely to be lucky in the quiet season between October and March.

INVERNESS STREET NW1

Inverness Street is just opposite the Camden Market site, but it's more of a local market dealing in food. if you want more details look it up in the Local Market section...

① PETE'S PLACE

② WKD CAFE

③ TASTY CORNER

④ NEW GOODFARE RESTAURANT

⑤ PARKWAY CAFE RESTAURANT

⑥ ITALIAN DELI

⑦ OASIS FOOD ARCH (VARIOUS STALLS)

ELECTRIC MARKET

Camden High Street

Open: Sunday 9am-5.30pm.

On Saturdays this indoor site holds the occasional record fair, but on Sundays its the regular venue for a second-hand clothes market. Here you can find a good range of weird and funky clothing but at rather inflated prices.

Getting a Stall

For further details phone Brian on 071 485 9006.

CAMDEN LOCK

North west of Camden Lock.

Open: Saturday-Sunday 10am-6pm.

The lock is the site where the whole Camden thing began in the early 70's. The warehouses have now been renovated into a kind of ethnic shopping centre with pine floors and arched windows. Inside are a great selection of fashionable clothes, arts and crafts and books. From here a huge complex of yards spreads westward with more clothes, books, hippy accessories and records and tapes on offer. If you find the choice just a little bewildering it's a good idea to clear your head and fill your stomach at the Oasis Food arch where every sort of food except English is served. It's quite difficult to find your way through this labyrinth so keep the map close to hand.

Getting a Stall

A lottery is held under the pedestrian bridge at 9.30am for a stall at the market. This is a pretty odd way of doing things and if you have a car load of goods you'll need someone to park while you wait in the queue for a place.

THE STABLES MARKET

West of Chalk Farm Road.

Open: Saturday-Sunday 9am-5pm.

The stables is the most northern part of Camden Market extending from the railway bridge to Chalk Farm tube. It's much the same as the lock with a good selection of groovy clothing, records and CDs and hippy accessories; but in addition there's a great deal of stylish furniture, lamps and antiques on offer. While some of the stuff is very good and there are always going to be some bargains in a place of this size, a lot of it is over priced. Similar lamps and furniture can be found cheaper south of the river in Greenwich.

Getting a Stall

Stalls are available on a first come basis from 7am and cost £15 for Saturdays and £30 for Sundays. If you want more details phone 071 482 2569.

Food & Drink

Although there are lots of good places to eat and drink in Camden many people congregate in and around MacDonalds on the High Street because they know what they're going to get. If you fancy being a little more adventurous, Parkway has the Tasty Corner for great coffee and cakes, the New Goodfare Restaurant for a good fry-up, and the eponymous Parkway Cafe for burgers. While you're there don't forget the great Italian Deli at no.30. If you like high cholesterol British grub, Pete's Place on Camden Road is a good greasy spoon. For those who want to see and be seen, the WKD Gallery Cafe on Kentish Town Road (behind Sainsbury's) plays great music and serves a pretty mean cappuccino.

4

Covent Garden Piazza
Tube: Covent Garden (Piccadilly)
Buses: 1, 6, 9, 11, 13, 15, 23, 77, 77A, 176 (Strand)
Open: Monday 9am-4pm (Antiques), Tuesday-Sunday 9am-4pm (Arts, Crafts & Souvenirs).

Until 1973 Covent Garden was the most famous of London's wholesale fruit and veg. markets. Nowadays there are three flourishing markets in and around the piazza. As they cater for tourists they're far from cheap and a lot of the stuff has only novelty value. Thousands of people must return home after visiting Covent Garden, unwrap their rainbow book ends and ceramic pigs and, in a more sober mood, ask "why?" One reason is that the market is great fun, particularly in the summer when the buskers are in full swing and the cafes full of people posing and enjoying the sun. If you're not concerned about the price of things, but just want to enjoy the crowds and window-shop, this is a great place to come. If you should find yourself returning home with a novelty toilet roll holder, remember you were warned...

Opera House Market (Clothes, New Ornaments, Arts & Crafts)

On Mondays this market is crammed with good quality, but expensive second-hand clothes. There are also a few stalls selling badges, jewellery and craft things. From Tuesday to Friday the market is given over to army surplus, cheap jewellery and African objects of dubious authenticity. At the weekend the market concentrates on crafts. It is here that essentials like Buddhist ritual symbols and the already mentioned novelty toilet roll holder can be found.

Apple Market (Antiques, Arts & Crafts)

On Mondays this market specializes in antiques. There are some beautiful objects on display, but nothing is under-priced. From Tuesday to Saturday the market sells well-made and fairly tasteful arts and crafts. The ubiquitous crockery pig is no stranger to this market, but you can also find hand-painted silk shirts and original colourful jumpers.

Jubilee Hall Market (Antiques, Souvenirs, Arts & Crafts)

Like the Apple Market, this hall specializes in antiques on Monday. From Tuesday to Friday all those with judgement should avoid this place. In the company of inflatable bananas, mugs with red buses on them and City of London T-shirts, even the crockery pig begins to look tasteful. On Saturday and Sunday the market is more crafts orientated, but still on the tacky side with things like illuminated pottery houses for £19 and flying stork mobiles for £13.99.

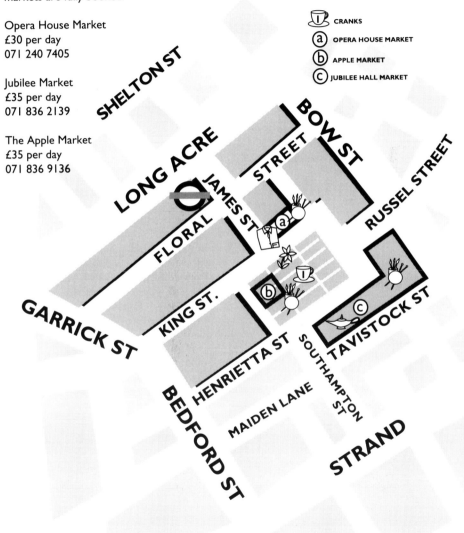

Getting a Stall
Covent Garden is just about as central as you can get so it's a good place to sell. If you visit the market any of the stall holders will direct you to the various market offices. Below are the telephone numbers to contact. It's best to phone first as many of the markets are fully booked.

Opera House Market
£30 per day
071 240 7405

Jubilee Market
£35 per day
071 836 2139

The Apple Market
£35 per day
071 836 9136

CRANKS
(a) OPERA HOUSE MARKET
(b) APPLE MARKET
(c) JUBILEE HALL MARKET

Greenwich Church Street, Stockwell Street, Greenwich High Road.
BR: Greenwich (London Bridge), Island Gardens (Docklands Light Railway - take foot tunnel to Greenwich).
Buses: 55, X53, 380 (Greenwich Park). 177, 180, 286 (Trafalgar Road). 188, 199 (Creek Road). 108 (Lewisham Road).
River Boat: This is a great way to visit Greenwich during the summer. Contact Greenwich Tourist Office on 081 858 6376 for further information, or visit any London tourist office and pick up a leaflet.
Open: Saturday-Sunday 9am-5pm.

Greenwich is the most happening market in London. If you're in search of good quality old and new clothes, furniture, antiques, music (CD's, tapes and records), as well as books and prints this is about the best place in London. Located on the Thames with seagulls, water and tourists it has the atmosphere of a seaside resort. Only the towering view of Canary Wharf across the river helps remind you that this is still London. Greenwich is a busy place, but it hasn't taken on the jaded atmosphere of Camden or Portobello.

However, there are signs that this is beginning to happen. One of the smaller less commercial parts of the market has become a garden centre, and a Burger King has replaced one of the long established junk shops on Greenwich Church Street. Your best course of action is to visit the place soon, before it inevitably deteriorates under the effect of its own success...

Bosun's Yard
Greenwich Church Street.
Open: Saturday-Sunday 9am-5pm.

This is a very well run indoor craft market. It hasn't got the range of the main craft market, but it does sell some things that the main market doesn't. One of the best buys was an entire wooden chess set with board for between £10 and £20 depending on size. Colourful hand painted silk cards were only £1.80, and framed prints were as little as £10. There's also a very good stall selling all sorts of pickles, mustards and flavoured cooking oils which make great presents for any foodie. On the subject of food there are several food stalls serving good stuff, but at tourist prices. You should be warned that this place is a claustrophobe's worst nightmare- small and busy. if you want to avoid the crush come early.

Getting a Stall
For details about trading here phone 081 293 4804 or visit the market in person.

The Flea Market
Thames Street
Open: Sunday 8am-4pm.

This part of Greenwich is often missed, being tucked away in a back street about five minutes walk from the busy centre. It is a strange place with traders selling their assortment of antiques, power tools, records, old clothes and bric-a-brac inside steel containers once used by ships. Walking through the covered area into the back yard you can combine sight seeing with pottering, getting one of the best views of Canary Wharf. One very important thing to note is the **parking** opposite the market. The traffic is pretty bad at the weekends, so it's a good idea to park here and walk along Thames Street into town...

Getting a Stall
For more information phone 081 305 2116.

ⓘ	TOURIST INFORMATION
1	THE MEETING POINT
2	ADMIRAL HARDY
3	THE COACH AND HORSES
4	USE YOU LOAF BAKERY
5	THE STUDIO BAR
6	TERMINUS COFFEE HOUSE
7	GODDARD'S PIE HOUSE
8	THAI OPEN AIR CAFE
9	INDOOR BOOK MARKETS

ⓐ	CAR BOOT SALE
ⓑ	BOSUN'S YARD
ⓒ	GREENWICH CENTRAL MARKET
ⓓ	ANTIQUES MARKET

Greenwich Antiques Market
Greenwich High Road.
Open: Saturday-Sunday 9am-5pm.

Although this part of Greenwich is called an antiques market it has only a few antiques along with a mixture of books, second-hand clothes, records and CD's, trendy jewellery, prints and the occasional crafts stall. The atmosphere is friendly and there are usually bargains to be found such as a glass paperweight for only £3.50 or a stylish hip length waterproof jacket for only £3. If you're thirsty the Studio Bar next door, is open pub hours and has seating outside in the summer. Greenwich Cinema is just a few doors down if you fancy an escape from the crowded streets.

Getting a Stall
Just turn up on the day of the market before 8.30am and ask to speak to the market manager Dennis.

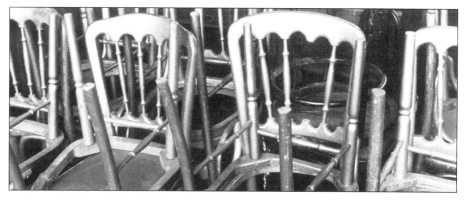

The Central Market

Stockwell Street.
Open: Saturday-Sunday 9am-5pm.

This is the largest market in Greenwich offering just about anything: kitsch things like a plastic crab, mountain bikes for £65, groovy second-hand and new clothes, furniture of all shapes, sizes and colours as well as two indoor book markets and many stalls selling records, CD's and books. The market is very roughly divided into three areas. To the east of the indoor book centre is a selection of bric-a-brac, antiques, books, tools and second-hand clothes. Behind the book centre lie most of the furniture stalls, one very well organized music stall, and a smattering of new clothes stalls. To the west are most of the stalls selling clothes. In the far left corner is an indoor section with clothes, furniture and antiques. Keep your eyes peeled for a brightly coloured van called The Mother Ship, where funky hair-cuts are just a fiver, try and get there early because it's always busy. The great Thai food stall is also in this part of the market, if you fancy something cheap and spicy. This part of Greenwich is worth a visit at any time of year, but is at it's best in the summer when you can combine shopping with catching a bit of sun...

Getting a Stall

Just turn up by 8am at the weekend and ask to speak to Frank the market manager.

The Craft Market

Greenwich Church Street, College Approach, King William Walk, Nelson Road.
Open: Saturday-Sunday 9am-5pm.

This place was a fruit and veg market for one hundred and fifty years and still has enshrined above the main entrance the words:
A FALSE BALANCE IS ABOMINATION TO THE LORD
BUT A JUST WEIGHT IS HIS DELIGHT.
Quite what the Lord would have made of the market's transformation into a craft centre is not certain, he might feel a little hurt by the stall offering astrological readings. There are lots of things at the market to tempt you, but there are few bargains. For a very well made and original man's top you'll have to pay between £15 and £20. For dresses the price is anything from £20 to £50. Bright hand painted ties are only £20, rather than the £35 charged in Covent Garden, and there is some very nice hand painted pottery at reasonable prices. One of the best buys can be found at the rug stall, a wool rug (3.5ft x 6ft) for only £22 - having paid over £100 for a similar one in IKEA this was a little upsetting. There are a number of good pubs within the market if you have had a similar shock, or just want a relaxing drink (see map for details).

Getting a Stall

For further details contact Bob O'Brien on 081 293 4224 or 081 293 3110.

PORTOBELLO ROAD W11

(6)

Portobello Road from (and including) Goldborne Road to Chepstow Villas.
Tube: Notting Hill Gate (Central, District, Circle). Ladbroke Grove (Metropolitan).
Buses: 12, 27, 28, 31, 52, 70, 94, 302 (Notting Hill Gate). 7, 23 (Ladbroke Grove).
Open: Antiques - Saturday 8.30am-5.30pm. General Mkt - Monday-Saturday 9am-5pm.

Like Camden market, Portobello isn't so much one market as five markets with different things to sell, and different opening times. Saturday is the big day for Portobello, when all the various parts of the market come together to form a mile of noise, colour and energy. If you're the sort of person who likes to shop till you drop then Saturday at Portobello is seventh heaven. On Sundays the streets are deserted and the only stalls open are those under the Westway, selling bric-a-brac, clothing and junk. It's a great day for a gentle wander, reading a paper in a quiet cafe, and perhaps a matinée at the Electric Cinema. During the week the only part of the market that's active is the central core of food stalls between Lonsdale Road and Lancaster Road. This is a great place to come for fresh fruit and veg, eggs and meat. If you're short of culinary inspiration there's always Books for Cooks on Blenheim Crescent, which also serves a pretty good coffee...

Getting a Stall
There are two bodies responsible for running market stalls:

1. The Local Council
Most of the market is run by Kensington & Chelsea Council (see Appendix).

2. Country Wide
071 221 4410
This company deals with all the stalls under the Westway. On Sundays the area under the Westway calls itself a Car Boot Sale, but is run by the same people (see P.69).

Food (Lonsdale Road-Lancaster Road)

Although grocery shopping isn't normally associated with Portobello Road this part of the market is excellent for all sorts of food - from the exotic to the essential. There's some excellent fruit and veg stalls with all sorts of fresh herbs at good prices - including large bunches of fresh mint for only 60p. Further along is the Applewold Farm Shop offering all sorts of fresh farm produce. If you need more basic food stuff there's a Tesco's just after the junction with Westbourne Park Road. Eve's Market Cafe, nextdoor to Tesco's, is a great place to stop for a fry-up or just a mug of tea.

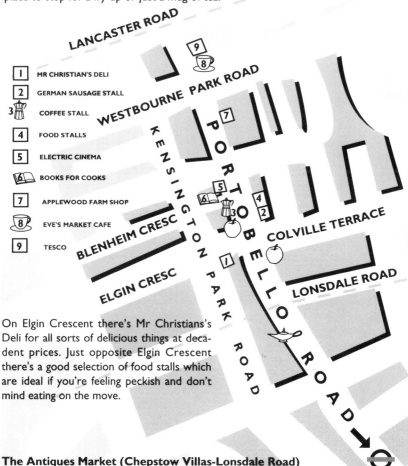

On Elgin Crescent there's Mr Christians's Deli for all sorts of delicious things at decadent prices. Just opposite Elgin Crescent there's a good selection of food stalls which are ideal if you're feeling peckish and don't mind eating on the move.

The Antiques Market (Chepstow Villas-Lonsdale Road)

This is the smart end of Portobello, largely catering for tourists and selling at tourist prices. The stalls and shops vary from the smart, organised and ultra expensive, to the pleasantly chaotic and moderately expensive. It's a great place to window shop and rummage, but you are very unlikely to find any bargains. It's worth remembering that this is the first stop for all those visiting the market by tube - many of them visiting the market for the first time and eager to get something. With such undiscriminating custom the stall holders can hardly be blamed for charging high prices.

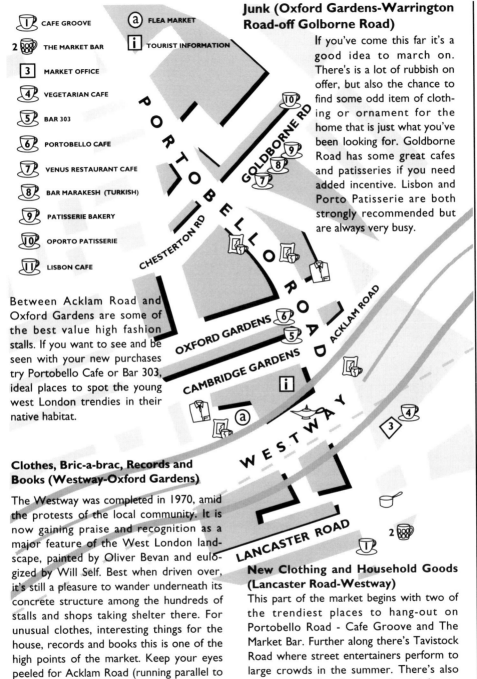

Legend

1. CAFE GROOVE
2. THE MARKET BAR
3. MARKET OFFICE
4. VEGETARIAN CAFE
5. BAR 303
6. PORTOBELLO CAFE
7. VENUS RESTAURANT CAFE
8. BAR MARAKESH (TURKISH)
9. PATISSERIE BAKERY
10. OPORTO PATISSERIE
11. LISBON CAFE

(a) FLEA MARKET
(i) TOURIST INFORMATION

Junk (Oxford Gardens-Warrington Road-off Golborne Road)

If you've come this far it's a good idea to march on. There's is a lot of rubbish on offer, but also the chance to find some odd item of clothing or ornament for the home that is just what you've been looking for. Goldborne Road has some great cafes and patisseries if you need added incentive. Lisbon and Porto Patisserie are both strongly recommended but are always very busy.

Between Acklam Road and Oxford Gardens are some of the best value high fashion stalls. If you want to see and be seen with your new purchases try Portobello Cafe or Bar 303, ideal places to spot the young west London trendies in their native habitat.

Clothes, Bric-a-brac, Records and Books (Westway-Oxford Gardens)

The Westway was completed in 1970, amid the protests of the local community. It is now gaining praise and recognition as a major feature of the West London landscape, painted by Oliver Bevan and eulogized by Will Self. Best when driven over, it's still a pleasure to wander underneath its concrete structure among the hundreds of stalls and shops taking shelter there. For unusual clothes, interesting things for the house, records and books this is one of the high points of the market. Keep your eyes peeled for Acklam Road (running parallel to the Westway) it's easily missed, but great for junk.

New Clothing and Household Goods (Lancaster Road-Westway)

This part of the market begins with two of the trendiest places to hang-out on Portobello Road - Cafe Groove and The Market Bar. Further along there's Tavistock Road where street entertainers perform to large crowds in the summer. There's also the market office if you need any information or help.

PETTICOAT LANE E1

(7)

Middlesex and Wentworth Street and all adjacent streets and lanes.
Tube: Aldgate (Metropolitan, Circle),
Aldgate East (District, Hammersmith & City), Liverpool Street (Circle, Central, Hammersmith and City, Metropolitan).
Buses: 8, 22A, 22B, 26, 35, 47, 48, 149, 505 (Liverpool Street Station).
5, 15, 15B, X15, 25, 40, 42, 67, 78, 100, 253 (Aldgate).
Open: All streets - Sunday 9am-2pm. Wentworth Street - Monday-Friday 10.30am-2.30pm.

Petticoat Lane is London's most famous market. Even on the wettest Sunday imaginable the place is packed. The market used to specialize in second-hand clothes, but now it's mostly new stuff. It's popularity doesn't make it the best value, but with over a thousand stalls on a Sunday you're bound to find some bargains.

As well as clothing, Petticoat Lane has a microphoned salesman on just about every corner trying to flog all manner of daft kitchen utensils. If you've ever lost a finger or arm in a carrot grating accident, you're probably in the market for one of these gadgets with built in guards to prevent such tragedies. If you prefer to grate on the wild side, just enjoy the free show. Another great spectacle of Petticoat Lane is the Christian sing-song at the north end of Middlesex Street. The preaching is not to everybody's taste, but it's worth waiting around to catch the funky music. If you're not so keen on the idea of washing your soul with the detergent of faith, the City Break Sandwich Bar is just next door.

The clothes at Petticoat Lane range from the tedious to the bizarre. On Middlesex Street chunky leather belts were only £5 (which is cheaper than anywhere else in London) and large nylon ruck sacks were as little as £3.99. At the far end of Leyden Street (on the corner with Stype Street) is one of the few stalls dealing in second-hand clothes, where you can find groovy suede jackets for the not unreasonable price of £14.99. On Wentworth Street there are some excellent clothes stalls offering Reeboks for £45, Peter Worth clothing, and some very good women's fashion. If you take a left and head south along Goulston Street you'll come to the Designer Market. In this enormous warehouse you can find just about every colour and style of leather jacket imaginable for between £60 and £180. Next to the indoor market is New Goulston Street where the playing of hard-core rap accompanies the selling of street cred clothing.

There are no end of places to eat and drink at Petticoat Lane. On Wentworth Street there's Vernasca Restaurant which does a good tea and fry-up. On the Junction with Bell Lane is Barcelona Tapas Bar if you fancy something a little different. John & Steve's Plaice on Toynbee Street does traditional fish & chips. Happy Days on Goulston Street is also a good place to stock up on cholesterol before tackling the crowds. For those who don't mind eating on the move the stall on Middlesex Street selling king prawns fried in garlic and butter is a real treat.

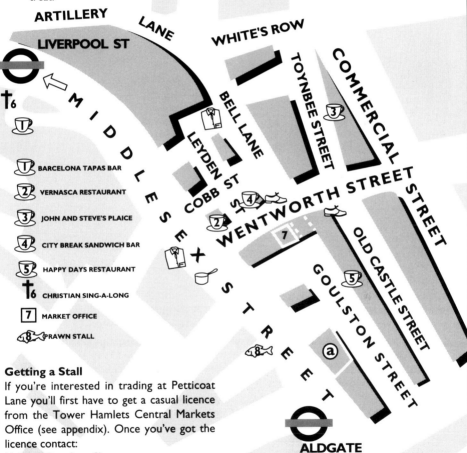

Key

1 BARCELONA TAPAS BAR
2 VERNASCA RESTAURANT
3 JOHN AND STEVE'S PLAICE
4 CITY BREAK SANDWICH BAR
5 HAPPY DAYS RESTAURANT
6 CHRISTIAN SING-A-LONG
7 MARKET OFFICE
8 PRAWN STALL

Getting a Stall

If you're interested in trading at Petticoat Lane you'll first have to get a casual licence from the Tower Hamlets Central Markets Office (see appendix). Once you've got the licence contact:
Holland One Stop Shop
29 Commercial Street
E1 6BD
071 375 0957
You may have to be patient though, because there's a waiting list to get a stall.

If you want a stall at the Designer Fashion Market on New Goulston Street contact Mr Spooner on 071 351 5353.

SPeCiALIst markets

SPECIALIST MARKETS

INTRODUCTION

The markets in this chapter are probably the most difficult to define but also the most interesting to explore. Breaking the markets down into sub-headings depending on their speciality is a good way to get a handle on this unruly bunch. The first section includes all those markets which deal in collectables or valuables of any kind. They're great fun to visit, if only to observe the rituals and customs of the greater spotted collector. Arts and crafts markets are also included within this section. Although many of them exist in a candle lit, incense burning world of their own, they can be good fun to visit - particularly if you have a fetish for Peruvian wool. The food markets in the second section are a good way to do the weekly shopping and enjoy yourself at the same time, while Columbia Road flower market is one of the best ways to spend a Sunday morning in London. Lunch-time markets deserve a section of their own simply because they all share the same pattern of business, quiet in the morning, hectic at mid day, dead or closed in the afternoon. They're good places to go for bargains, and a fun way to spend a spare lunch-time. The Sunday markets are nothing out of the ordinary except for the fact that being on a Sunday they tend to have a slightly more relaxed atmosphere, with lots of families making the most of the day of rest before the rigours of Monday morning.

Arts Crafts antiQues & Books

BAYSWATER ROAD & PICCADILLY MARKET (W2 & W1)

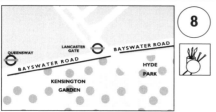

South side of Bayswater Road from Albion Gate to Queensway. South side of Piccadilly from Queen's Walk to Hyde Park Corner.
Tube: Lancaster Gate (Central). Green Park (Victoria, Piccadilly and Jubilee).
Buses: 8, 9, 14, 19, 22, 38 (Piccadilly). 12, 70, 94 (Bayswater Road).
Open: Sunday 9.30am-4pm.

Every Sunday hundreds of artists (I use the word broadly) line the pavement of Bayswater and Piccadilly to display their work. Most of the paintings are directly representational and concentrate on a very limited number of themes. There are lots of pictures of rural idylls with titles such as "Early Morning Mist", "Tranquill Dawn" and "Mice in Cornfield". Typical London scenes such as Big Ben, bright red buses and friendly smiling beefeaters are another favourite. Rex Wingfield was not alone in depicting healthy young ladies in a rural setting. His canvas "Waiting for Her Fisherman" captures the latent desire of a girl with far more than EEC fishing quotas on her mind. Bill Holkham demonstrates slightly better hand to eye coordination, but equal monomania with his oil paintings of World War II allied fighter and bomber planes, a firm favourite with German visitors to the capital. Interspersed with the paintings you'll find essentials like woolly toilet roll holders, pictures made from clock parts and metal sculptures of skeletons playing musical instruments. A walk along Bayswater and Piccadilly is a fun way to spend a free Sunday. If you're peckish try Shepherd's Market square, just north of Piccadilly, which has lots of good cafes such as the Village Coffee Shop and Gigi's, both of which are open on Sundays.

Getting a Stall
For more details contact Westminster City Council (see appendix).

BERMONDSEY (NEW CALEDONIAN) MARKET SE10

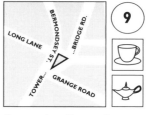

Bermondsey Square, between Abbey Street, Bermondsey Street, and Tower Bridge Road.
Tube: Borough (Northern), Elephant & Castle (Bakerloo).
Buses: 1, 42, 78, 188, 199 (Tower Bridge Road). 21, 53, 63, 171, 172, 177 (Great Dover Street).
Open: Friday 5am-1pm.

This is London's largest and, if you're lucky, best value antiques market. Antique dealers have been cramming this small square of South East London with rare and wonderful objects since 1949, when the market moved from Copenhagen Fields in Islington. The place still has a reputation for the sale of dodgy goods, which really comes from it's distant past when things were sold from blankets on the pavement. It's a lot more respectable now. Most of the stall holders these days are eager to have their stall photographed for the publicity, rather than the shady camera shy figures of Bermondsey mythology.

Trading is well under way by 5am, as dealers do business with each other by torch light. Rumour has it that much of the trade at this time is destined for the morning ferry crossing to adorn Continental antique shops where it collects a very high price. By 9am trade business is done and quite a few of the stalls pack up. With an increasing number of tourists making their way across the river to see what all the fuss is about, many stalls stay until lunch time to cater for them. Most of the traders at Bermondsey are full-time dealers and know the value of their most precious items, but it's still possible to find attractive things very cheaply. A beautiful Orientalist style oil canvas depicting an Arab bazaar was only £35. A small very well made teddy bear of uncertain age was only £8, and a very neat little chess set was only £6. None of these items were genuine antiques, but they were attractive and good value. If you want genuine antiques at Bermondsey you'll need a considerable amount of money and sufficient knowledge to distinguish the genuine from the fake.

There are a great many places to get nourishment around the market. Bill's van is always there dispensing hot tea and fried food to revive the flagging bargain hunter. On Market Bridge Street there's The Market Cafe and further south M. Manze Pie and Mash shop. Rose's Diner on Bermondsey Street is an old favourite.

Getting a Stall
For more information contact Southwark Council (see appendix).

CAMDEN PASSAGE N1

On the junction of Essex Road and Upper Street, next to Islington Green.
Tube: Angel (Northern)
Buses: 4, 19, 30, 38, 43, X43, 73, 171A, 56, 279 (Islington Green).
Open: (Antiques) Wednesday 7am-2pm, Saturday 8am-4pm.
(Books) Thursday 7am-4pm.

There are two surprising things about Camden Passage. Firstly it's not in Camden, but in Islington. It was named after the Earl of Camden - Charles Pratt. A fortuitous choice of name all things considered. Secondly, the antiques market is not centuries old as you might think, but started in 1960 when Islington became trendy and expensive.

The antiques market is a great place to wander round. The stalls are crammed with objects from the kitsch to the beautiful - black 1930's phones for £30, a set of 1920 flying ducks for £65 and a wonderful Victorian writing slope for £170. The stall holders are pretty knowledgeable and very willing to talk at great length and detail about the rarity and worth of their goods. For this reason, and because of the popularity of the market, you are unlikely to find many bargains. Even the tackiest object is seldom less than £5. For those with just enough money to afford a cappuccino at one of the expensive cafes in the area it's still worth a visit just to look. At the Islington High Street end of Camden Passage a small and easily missed book market takes place every Thursday. On offer is a good selection of paperback fiction and reference books. It's a great place to browse if you want to escape the hubbub of the High Street.

Getting a Stall
Wednesday is the busiest day and the cost of a stall is £20. On Thursday and Saturday they're only £15. For further details contact Sara Lemkow on 071 359 0190 or call into her shop at 12 Camden Passage.

CHARING CROSS COLLECTOR'S FAIR WC2

Villiers Street - underneath Embankment tube station.
Tube: Embankment (Northern, Barkerloo, District and Circle).
Charing Cross/BR (Northern, Jubilee, Bakerloo).
Buses: 3, 3B, 6, 9, 11, 12, 13, 15, 23, 24, 29, 53, 77A, 88, 91, 94, 109, 139, 159, 176.
Open: Saturday 8.30am-5pm.

Collectors are a strange breed. Like many shy retiring creatures, they are rarely seen in their natural habitat. This subterranean gathering every Saturday allows you to observe them in the process of hoarding those objects which are dear to them. It's here that an assortment of coins, medals, badges and stamps change hands, amid the inhaling of tobacco smoke, the scratching of beard, and the long (some might say interminable) exposition of the one that got away. For the collector and anthropologist alike it's worth a visit.

Getting a Stall
It's £20 for a table at the fair. For more details contact Rodney on 081 398 8065.

FARRINGDON ROAD EC1

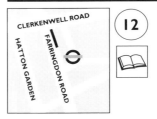

Farringdon Road (Between Clerkenwell Road and Cowcross Street).
Tube: Farringdon (Circle, Metropolitan).
Buses: 5, 55 (Clerkenwell Road). 63, 168A, 221, 243, 259 (Farringdon Road)
Open: Monday-Friday 10am-2pm.

Heavy traffic has put an effective end to the days when this was a flourishing book market. All that remains are the three stalls run by Mr Jeffery, who still keeps a smile on his face despite the weather and the carbon monoxide. Amongst the assortment of books and prints on offer there's plenty of interest. If you're in the area take a look.

Getting a Stall
This is really a bit of a one-man show. If you want to sell books look in the item index for other markets worth trying.

HAMPSTEAD COMMUNITY MARKET NW3

Hampstead High Street.
Tube: Hampstead (Northern).
Buses: 46, 268 (High Street)
Open: Saturdays 9.30am-6pm.

Hampstead is full of posh cars, smart boutiques (including one for children), cafes and writers. This is just the sort of place you wouldn't expect to find an interesting market, and you'd be right. The atmosphere is that of a village fete complete with craft goods, books and records, all at inflated prices. It does have a cafe, but the tables are in the middle of the small hall forcing the shopper and eater into unhappy intimacy. There are some good permanent stalls to the side of the community centre selling fresh fish, pet food and fruit and veg, but nothing is cheap.

Getting a Stall

Phone Richard Weaver on 071 794 8313 for further details.

MERTON ABBEY MILLS SW19

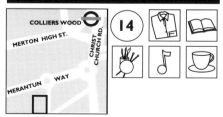

Off Merantum Way, behind the Savacentre.
Tube: Colliers Wood (Northern).
Buses: 93, 293 (Morden Road). 219, 293 (Colliers Wood). 57, 152, 155 (Merton High Street).
Open: Saturday-Sunday 10am-5pm.

Merton Abbey is called a "Craft Village", but all the stalls that pitch here during the weekend are run by the same kind of itinerant traders that do business in Camden or Greenwich. The market is a good one and well worth a visit, what grates is the contrived nature of the place, the fact that it makes claim to being "rich in history" and some sort of throw back to "ye olde England" when it's nothing of the sort. What Merton Abbey does have is the River Wandle flowing by its side, and more fresh air than you have a right to expect from a market only twenty minutes tube journey from the city. With up to 200 stalls on a Sunday and permanent shops offering books, records and good quality arts and crafts the place offers a good opportunity to get away from the smog of the city and have a potter in suburbia.

Abbey Mills has its fair share of esoteric stalls, there's also the usual range of craft market clobber. But in addition it has some interesting goods which make it worth visiting. The best thing about the market is the range of clothes made by independent designers. One stall sold handmade bomber jackets for between £70 and £90, you could even have a jacket made to your own design and ready within a week, which seemed a pretty good deal. There were also some funky hats for as little as £6, matching cotton long johns and top for £22, and full sleeve cotton tops for only £5.

On Sundays there are lots of refreshment stalls offering anything from Thai noodles to carrot cake and coffee. If you want to rest your feet there's the tea house which is usually busy, or the pizza restaurant which affords you a great view of the river as you tuck into your traditional English Deep Pan Pizza...

Getting a Stall

Speaking to some of the stall holders, this sounds like a good place to trade. For more details phone 081 543 9608.

SPECIALIST MARKETS

PICCADILLY MARKET W1

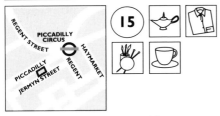

St James's Church Yard, Piccadilly.
Tube: Piccadilly Circus (Piccadilly, Bakerloo).
Green Park (Victoria, Jubilee, Piccadilly)
Buses: 9, 14, 19, 22, 38 (Piccadilly).
Open: Friday-Saturday 10am-5pm.

On Fridays and Saturdays you can combine sight seeing with shopping in the courtyard of St James's Church. The market contains antiques, jewellery both old and new, thick wool jumpers for only £30, a stall selling interesting second-hand clothes at inflated prices, and another specializing entirely in pipes. If consumer durables aren't your thing you can always indulge in a bag of hand made fudge for only 75p or visit the great cafe in the church annex. The courtyard is surprisingly green and pleasant, an excellent place to chill if you've had enough of the West End.

Getting a Stall
For details visit the Rector's Office or phone 071 734 4511.

PLATTS MARKET SE1

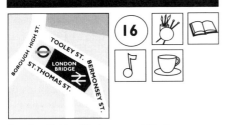

London Bridge Underground Station.
BR/Tube: London Bridge (Northern, Network SouthEast).
Buses: 17, 21, 22A, 35, 40, 43, X43, 47, 48, 133, 344 (London Bridge).
Open: Saturday 10am-4.30pm.

On Saturdays the normal hustle and bustle of London Bridge station makes room for about fifteen craft, memorabilia, CD, book, and souvenir stalls. Most of the trade comes from those who are passing through or awaiting the arrival of a loved one. It isn't really worth going out of your way to visit, but if "leaves on the track" leave you stranded it's a great place to while away the time. The cafe also serves a great cappuccino if you're a bit parched.

Getting a Stall
For details ring Rodney on 081 398 8065.

THE COURTYARD WC2

St Martin's Church Yard, St Martin's Place.
BR/Tube: Charing Cross.
Buses: 3, 6, 9, 11, 12, 13, 15, 23, 24, 53, 77A, 88, 91, 94, 139, 159 (Trafalgar Square).
Open: Monday-Saturday 11am-6.30pm.

This central London market caters largely for the many tourists wandering from Trafalgar Square to the National Gallery. The only Londoners you find within the environs of the courtyard are the stall holders and the homeless who queue in the afternoon for shelter in the crypt of St Martin's Church. Not all the clothes and craft goods on offer are rubbish, but the good quality things are overpriced. If you enter from behind the church (Adelaide Street) most of the horrendous souvenir stuff is avoided. There are a few reasonable stalls selling food, and places to sit. If you're really lucky the gentleman running the book stall might give you a rendition of Green Sleeves on his penny whistle!

Getting a Stall
For details ring Arthur on 071 930 7821.

Food & Flowers

BERWICK STREET W1

Berwick Street, from Broadwick Street extending south on to Rupert Street.
Tube: Oxford Circus (Victoria, Central), Piccadilly Circus (Bakerloo, Piccadilly), Tottenham Court Road (Northern).
Buses: 7, 8, 10, 55, 73, 98, 176 (Oxford Street). 14, 19, 23, 38, 53, X53, 88, 94, 139, 159 (Shaftesbury Avenue).
Open: Monday-Saturday 9am-5pm.

Berwick Street Market dates back to the 1840's, when there was still a market near Oxford Circus. Oxford Street is now a nightmare of tourists and traffic; but Berwick Street and its market have managed to keep a great deal of their character. The stall holders still call for their trade, some making noises beyond the comprehension of any human ear simply for their own amusement. In recent times they have been forced to compete with the burgeoning array of record shops in the street. The market largely specialises in fruit and veg. The prices and the quality vary from stall to stall, so it's worth looking around before you buy. Berwick Street has a good range of produce - if you're looking for fresh herbs or an unusual vegetable you should be able to get them from one of the stalls.

One thing the prospective punter should keep in mind is that fruit grows on trees and money does not. In other words, if a stall holder is selling something at a very cheap price it may not be fresh. So always check the quality before dishing out your dosh.

Berwick Street is not only a good place to find an organic mushroom or tender courgette. It also possesses an excellent fresh fish stall, and others specializing in cheese, herbs and spices, household goods and fabrics. Complementing the foodie nature of the market, "Simply Sausages" at 93 Berwick street, sells the best selection of sausages in town. The Algerian Coffee store on Old Compton street is well worth a visit for all manner of fresh tea and coffee. There's also an amazing choice of Italian deli's in and around Berwick Street reflecting the streets cosmopolitan history.

Don't forget that there are more stalls if you carry on south through the passageway into Rupert Street. Here you can find more fruit and veg along with a mixture of clothing, small electrical and souvenir stalls most of which are over priced and of dubious quality. Tisbury Court on the left, has some good trendy clothes shops, although the prices charged may encourage you to maintain a more conservative dress code.

Unfortunately Berwick Street doesn't boast a great cafe or restaurant. The Berwick Street Snack Bar is cheap and cheerful, there are a few burger bars and a fish and chip shop, but nothing special. For lentil heads there's Cranks on Marshall Street, which is pleasant but pricy.

Getting a Stall
Contact Westminster City Council about either Berwick or Rupert Street (see appendix).

CHAPEL MARKET N1

Between Liverpool Road and Penton Street.
Tube: Angel (Northern).
Buses: 4, 19, 30, 38, 43, X43, 56, 73, 171A, 279 (Islington High Street). 153 (Pentonville Road).
Open: Tuesday, Wednesday, Friday and Saturday 9am-5pm. Thursday and Sunday 9am-12.30pm.

Chapel Market is one of the best things about Islington. It's been on the street for over a hundred years. On Saturday and Sunday it covers the entire length of the street. The fruit and veg is good quality and value, but you won't find anything out of the ordinary - no yams or cassavas. Likewise, the fresh fish stall is excellent, with mackerel for 80p per lb and lemon sole at £2.90lb, but red snapper or blue runner are strangers here. It's a good place to come for consumer durables of all sorts - basic clothes, pots, pans, cushions, bedding, bags of all shapes and sizes, as well as a music stall offering the Barry Manilow compilation for only £2.50!

White Conduit Street is an interesting diversion from the market. There's a junk shop which sells anything from a Moulinex Mixer (£15), to sheet music. Nicholette's has new things for the home - vases, glasses, kitchen utensils, Neal's Yard toiletries, along with wrapping paper and cards. It's expensive, but a great place for gifts. Next door is Tony's cafe, where a full breakfast will set you back only £2.20. Cafes and restaurants worthy of special mention are Alpino's at 97 Chapel street for its cheap pasta dishes, the Bhel Poori House for great value vegetarian Indian food, and the baked potato stall on the corner of Chapel place.

Chapel Street also has a good range of shops in the surrounding area. On Liverpool Road there's a large Sainsbury's, and a small deli called Barstow and Bar which specializes in cheese. On Chapel Street itself there's a Marks and Spencer's, Superdrug and Woolworth's. Last but by no means least is Olga Stores on Penton Street, which is the only Italian deli in the area, and well worth a visit.

Getting a Stall
Contact Islington Council (see appendix).

COLUMBIA ROAD MARKET E2

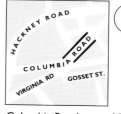

Columbia Road east of Ravenscroft Street.
Tube: Old Street (Northern). Bethnal Green (Central).
Buses: 26, 48, 55 (Hackney Road).
Open: Sunday 8am-12.30pm.

Columbia Road Market is a great place to see fauna in search of flora. The eager Sunday gardener can wander (or rather push their way) through the throng in pursuit of the interesting or the bizarre, and will seldom emerge disappointed. It's a good idea to begin from the southern approach to the market, with the prospect of coffee and a rest at the cafe on Ezra Street to encourage you in your struggle against the hordes.

For those readers that are more interested in a calceolaris than a coffee, there are one or two things to bear in mind before parting with your dosh. All small plants are sold in trays of approximately 20 plants. This is economical if you are looking to flower a medium to large garden. It is not so good for those with small gardens or just a humble flower box. So don't go bonkers or you may find yourself with more plants and less money than you intended. Carrying a great many plants through the hubbub of Columbia Road can be quite a task. It's a good idea to take a bag with you; but if you forget they can be bought cheaply (around £2) at the market. The stall holders are inevitably rushed off their feet and will not have the time to give you all the advice you might need. Go prepared to the market with some idea of the plants you want. Remember, the better prepared you are the less likely you are to make a mistake. The plants at Columbia Road are very good value, but if you're looking for real bargains wait till the end of the day, when the cut flowers and quite a few of the pot plants are being sold off cheaply. However, if you want to avoid the crush then get there as early as possible. The market starts at 8.00am, so that those early birds amongst you can visit the market, buy your plants, have a coffee and a pastry and still get home in time for Gardeners' Question Time...

Getting a Stall

First you'll have to get a casual licence from the Tower Hamlets Central Markets Office (see appendix). Once you've got the licence contact:
Columbia One Stop Shop
29 Columbia Road E2
071 739 7545

SPITALFIELDS E1

West side of Commercial Street between Folgate and Brushfield Street.
Tube: Liverpool Street (Central, Metro & Circle lines).
Buses: 5, 67, N84 (Commercial Street) 6, 8, 22, 35, 47, 48, 78, 149 (Bishopsgate).
Open: food and shops Monday-Friday 9am-6pm & weekends. Market open 11am-3pm Sunday.

Until recently this incredible five acre warehouse was one of London's largest wholesale fruit, veg and flower markets. It's now an entertainment and shopping centre, with a small sports complex, smart shops, restaurants and great food stalls. Fruit and veg are still sold here on Sundays at the organic food market along with free range farm eggs, fresh bread, pastries and homemade jams and chutneys. If you like to know what you eat, the meat stall displays photos of the cattle with captions telling you their names. Along with all the delicious food there are stalls offering hats, candlesticks, essential oils, as well as the occasional bric-a-brac stall. If this all proves too much, you can always treat yourself to a head massage for a couple of quid. Another attraction is the mechanical railway sculpture, which is great fun to watch when it springs into musical life every 15 minutes.

Getting a Stall

It's free during the week and £20 on a Sunday. Contact Karen Brown on 071 247 6590 for more details.

Lunch-Time Markets

CHARLTON STREET NW1

Between Euston Road and Phoenix Road.
Tube: Euston (Northern, Victoria). King's Cross (Piccadilly, Metropolitan, Circle).
Buses: 10, 14, 17, 30, 68, 73, 91, 168, 214, 259 (central).
Open: Monday-Friday 12pm-2pm.

This weekday lunch-time market is only really busy on Fridays. Thousands of people pass by along the Euston Road, but few have reason to stop. It's a pity because among the cheap cleaning fluids and nylon bedding there are some great bargains. Men's designer clothes are only a fraction of the retail price. Kitchen equipment such as pots and pans are good value, and the shoe stall sells DM boots for only £35. The street also has its fair share of cafes, the best being Linores Sandwich Bar where you can get a great lunch for only £3. As the British Library nears completion, hopefully more people will find a chance to visit this forgotten backwater.

Getting a Stall
For further details contact Camden Council (see appendix).

LEADENHALL EC3

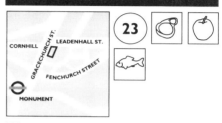

Whittington Avenue, off Gracechurch and Leadenhall Street.
Tube: Bank (Central, Northern). Monument (Circle, District).
Buses: 15B, X15, 25 (Leadenhall Street). 22A, 25, 35, 47, 48, 505 (Gracechurch Street). 8, 22B, 26, 149 (Bishopsgate).
Open: Monday-Friday 7am-4pm.

In 1881 Leadenhall Arcade was completed. Designed by Sir Horace Jones, made of cast-iron and stone, it has kept its charm, as well as many of the original shop fronts. Exactly one hundred years later and about twenty yards to the North-East, work began on the new Lloyds Building, designed by Richard Rogers and made of concrete and stainless steel. The contrast isn't as bad as it sounds. It does at least afford you the chance to stand in Leadenhall Place and watch people in suits ascend and descend the Lloyds Building in glass lifts.

The market (consisting of a handful of shops with stalls extending onto the pavement) specializes in fresh fish, poultry, meat and fruit and veg. The quality is very good, but the prices are high. The cafes in and around the market are of the stand up/polystyrene cup variety. The pubs are smart, serve good beer and are packed at lunch-time with people in pin-stripe suits. Despite its drawbacks, Leadenhall market is worth a visit. The best time to go is Christmas when the arcade is festooned with poultry and delicacies for the festive season.

Getting a Stall
All the stalls at Leadenhall are run on a leasehold basis. Look in the subject index for other markets specializing in food.

LEATHER LANE EC1

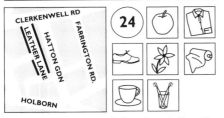

Between Clerkenwell Road and Greville Street.
Tube: Farringdon (Circle, Metropolitan), Chancery Lane (Central).
Buses: 8, 17, 22B, 25, 45, 46, 171A (Holborn). 55 (Clerkenwell Road).
Open: Monday-Friday 10.30am-2pm.

While Exmouth market has suffered in the last 20 years as a result of redevelopment, Leather Lane has thrived. Between 10.30 and 12pm the street is very quiet. By 12.15 it's packed with the work force of Holborn in desperate search of bargains and groceries in their lunch-hour. By 2.15 even the most work shy clerk has returned to his desk, and the market starts to close. With a good selection of fruit and veg, new clothes, shoes, toiletries, plants and cloth by the yard, the market is well worth a visit. If you want to avoid the crush come early. At the Clerkenwell end of the market you can treat yourself to last months glossy mags at 3 for £1.00. Men's jogging/casual trousers - which are £20 in Camden - can be found here for only £15, and long cotton dresses are as little as £10. The plant stall has a reasonable selection, but if you want a bargain you'll have to wait until the end of the day when the less durable specimens are reduced to clear.

One of the best things about Leather Lane is the range of shops, cafes and restaurants in the area. L.Terroni & Sons, on Clerkenwell Road, is just about the best Italian deli in town. Ferraro Continental Stores is another great little shop for high quality food. Among the best places to eat are Collin's Nest for tea, coffee and fried food, and Diana's Dining Room for more elaborate meals and snacks. There are two kosher cafes on Granville Street catering for the Jewish community centred around the diamond trade of Hatton Gardens. The courtyard of Holborn Bars is on your right as you walk from the market through the pedestrian shopping area. It's open to the public, and a great place to catch your breath after the chaos of the market.

Getting a Stall
For further details contact Camden Council (see appendix).

LOWER MARSH STREET SE1

Lower Marsh from Westminster Bridge Road to Baylis Road.
Tube: Waterloo (Northern, Bakerloo).
Buses: 1, 4, 26, 68, 76, 77, 176 (Waterloo). 12, 53, 109, 184 (Westminster Bridge Road).
Open: Monday-Saturday 10am-2pm.

This market used to be a lot bigger, stretching across Waterloo Road and along The Cut. It's still a good size with over a hundred stalls on its busiest days (Tuesday, Thursday and Friday). On offer is a good selection of fruit and veg, LP's and tapes for £2, kitchen and electrical equipment, trendy trainers, potted plants, cut flowers and new clothes. On the left-hand side as you walk from Westminster Bridge Road there's a small privately run courtyard which sells good quality material for less than £2 per yard. Unlike many Englishmen, the man with the underwear stall brazenly declares the quality and value of his garments, with bargains like six pairs of ladies undies for £3, you can hardly blame him. There are also some interesting and unusual shops on the street. Twice the Siren at No.28 is full of unusual and expensive women's clothes. The Eastern Supermarket at no.119 is a great place to find herbs and spices. For the kinky and those who like to snigger awkwardly at rude things there's always Honour- Rubber Fantasy at no.86. Gramex, next door, is one of the best classical music shops in London, and just opposite is Ian Allan book shop specializing in military and transport matters. Streets Cafe-Bar is a good place to hang out with the paper and a beverage of your choice.

Getting a Stall

For more details about trading at the main market contact:
Lower Marsh Market Office
Baylis Road SE1
071 928 6851 between 3-4pm.
For a stall in the courtyard contact:
Charlie Samuel
132 Lower Marsh Street.
071 928 7782

STRUTTON GROUND SW1

The south side of Victoria Street.
Tube: St James's Park (Circle, District).
Buses: 11, 24, 507, 511 (Victoria Street).
Open: Monday-Friday 11.30am-3pm.

This is not the world's largest or most exciting market. It offers the usual selection of fruit and veg stalls, cheap new clothing and household goods, catering for those who work in the towering office blocks of Victoria Street. The thing that's interesting about the place is its location amid all the chaos of modern metropolitan life. If you're hungry there are also many places to eat such as Barclay's for a traditional cholesterol soaked fry-up, the Laughing Halibut for fish and chips, as well as Rossana's cafe-bar, and the Exchange Wine Bar for those who like a more genteel atmosphere. Stiles the bakery is another reason for venturing into this narrow road, if only to catch a whiff of fresh baked bread. Take the opportunity to see Westminster Cathedral further along Victoria Street, it's one of the most beautiful buildings in London.

Getting a Stall

For further details contact Westminster Council (see appendix).

WHITECROSS STREET EC1

Whitecross Street between Old Street and Fortune Street.
Tube: Barbican (Circle and Metropolitan) Old Street (Northern).
Buses: 55, 243 (Old Street).
4, 172 (Aldersgate St).
43, X43, 76, 133, 141, 172, 214, 271 (City Road).
Open: Monday-Friday 10.30am-2.30pm.

Situated in the shadow of the new Barbican Centre, this is a great lunch-time market. There's lots on offer-crockery, cheap linen and towels, small electrical things and a good range of new clothes. You can also find reasonable bags, shoes and linen at the southern end of the market in the shelter of the indoor shopping arcade. The street is lined with cheap and cheerful cafes - all of which are packed at lunch-time. There are also a great many pubs, reflecting the markets history as the site of the Whitbread brewery. At the far end of the street lies a small park (access through Shrewsbury court or Fortune Street) where you can escape from the bustle of the market, inspect your purchases, and look up at the three imposing towers of the Barbican Complex.

Getting a Stall

Contact Islington Council for details (see appendix).

Sunday Markets

EARL'S COURT SUNDAY MARKET SW5

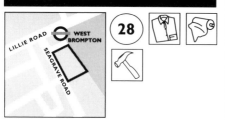

Open-air car-park Seagrave Road.
Tube/BR: West Brompton (District).
Buses: 31, 74, C1, C3 (Earl's Court).
Open: Sunday 9am-2pm.

This Sunday market remains popular with the local Arab community, and several stalls specialize in arabic literature and videos. Also on offer are good quality wool rugs, trendy mainstream women's clothing, a good value underwear stall offering men's boxer shorts for only £2 each, cheap tools at the hardware stall and simple fabrics for only £2 per yard. Unfortunately the jewellery, watches and toys were cheap but not very good quality, and one stall holder did himself no favours putting up a sign saying "I have time only for people with money". Due to the demands of the conference centre the market is closed about one Sunday a month, so it's a good idea to check in the local press or phone the market operators (see below) before making your way here.

Getting a Stall
For more details contact Hughmark International on 0734 451 799.

NINE ELMS SUNDAY MARKET SW8

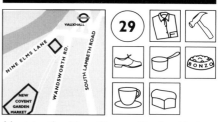

Next to the New Covent Garden Market, Nine Elms Lane.
Tube/BR: Vauxhall (Victoria).
BR: Battersea Park.
Buses: 44, 344 (Nine Elms Lane). 77, 77A, 322 (Wandsworth Road).
Open: Sunday 9am-2pm.

Pitched in the concrete maze of New Covent Garden, and encircled by major roads, this market is best reached by car. Here you can find cheap clothing, basic DIY equipment, very cheap nylon ruck sacks, shoes, videos ranging from the popular to the obscure, pet food, kitchen equipment and a stall selling sweet pastries and bread. Most of the stuff is of questionable quality and taste, but there were some good buys to be had - such as Doc Martin shoes for only £20 and woman's cotton tops for only £3.99. With fast food stalls everywhere you look and Radio One competing with the generators for airspace, this is a market for those who think Sunday is anything but a day of rest.

Getting a Stall
Nine Elms market is privately run. For more details contact Mr Nunan of Bray Associates on 0895 639 912.

WEMBLEY SUNDAY MARKET HA9

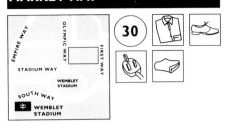

Stadium Way, Wembley, Middlesex.
Tube: Wembley Park (Metropolitan).
BR: Wembley Stadium.
Open: Sunday 9am-2pm.

If you wanted proof that Britain is a nation of shopkeepers (and shoppers), Wembley Sunday market is a good first stop. Even on cold, windy days the thoroughfares dividing the 500 or more stalls are packed with bargain hunters. The smell of hot dogs, the hum of the generators and the eager crowds give the place a carnival atmosphere.

On offer are clothes, towels and linen, tools, electrical goods, tacky jewellery, carpets, bags and basic foods. Most of the goods aren't top quality, but if you hunt around you can find some good buys. Chunky wool jumpers were only £19.95, Dr Martin shoes could be found for only £30, with the best value award going to the bag stall selling good quality nylon back packs for only £2. If you're looking for a laugh join the crowd in front of Michael Levy's towel and linen stall. This man is so good at selling he runs courses in how to do it. With a technique only rivalled by the awesome "Mr Meat" at Brick Lane.

The worst thing about this market is the traffic. Car park prices varied from £6 at the main car park to £2 for one just around the corner, so it's worth looking around before parking.

Getting a Stall
A stall here costs £60, so think about it before committing yourself. For further details contact:
Wendy Fairs   0895 675 558.

LoCal MaRKETS

INTRODUCTION

London can be a pretty daunting, hostile place, full of strangers. Local markets are a good way to see a different side of the city because each one reflects a different community. Here you'll find Londoners in their native habitat, bargain hunting, shopping for the week's groceries or just having a natter. The markets vary greatly depending on the communities which give them life. For example, Ridley Road has a good mix of West Indian, Asian, Turkish and European food, reflecting the diversity of Dalston's population. While Queen's Crescent is a real meeting place for the residents of Kentish Town.

These markets aren't just for anthropological study, they're also excellent places to look for bargains. Household basics like crockery and bedding are usually found at well below shop prices, and the occasional second-hand stall can yield the odd gem if you're lucky. Although most local markets are open during the week it's important to take note of the busiest days. Markets like Hoxton and Chrisp Street are buzzing on a Friday or Saturday, but dead as a dodo the rest of the week.

BALHAM MARKET SW12

Hildreth Street
Tube: Balham (Northern Line).
Buses: 88 (central), 155, 355 (local).
Open: Monday-Saturday 9.30am-5pm.
Thursdays 9.30am-1pm.

This small pedestrian street has held a market since 1903. The mix of continental food stores, fish mongers and butchers complement the pitches selling toiletries, kitchen ware, fresh eggs and a good selection of fruit and veg. Across the road on Bedford Hill is a small indoor market. There's little to buy in this run down building, but, with three Jamaican take-aways, plenty to eat. If you fancy a fry-up, Dot's Cafe on Hildreth Street gets the thumbs up.

Getting a Stall
Contact Wandsworth Council for further details (see appendix).

BATTERSEA HIGH STREET SW11

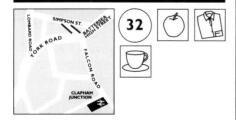

South end of Battersea High Street.
BR: Clapham Junction (Victoria, Waterloo).
Buses: 44, 344 (central).
Open: Monday-Saturday 9.30am-4.30pm.

A small pedestrian market offering the usual selection of fruit and veg, tinned foods, cards and clothes. Notarianni & Sons and Jack Hall's are both worth a visit if you're feeling peckish.

Getting a Stall
For further details contact Wandsworth Council (see appendix).

BETHNAL GREEN ROAD E2

South side of Bethnal Green Road from Vallance Road to Wilmot Street.
Tube: Bethnal Green (Central).
Buses: 8 (Bethnal Green Road). 106, 253, D6 (Cambridge Heath).
Open: Monday-Saturday 8.30am-5pm.
Thursday 8.30-12.30.

This is a friendly market serving the local community. The market is at it's biggest and best on Friday and Saturday, stretching from Vallance Road to Wilmot Street. On offer is the usual fare of new clothes, toiletries, cleaning materials, cloth by the yard, fruit and veg, eggs, fresh fish and a good value meat stall. There are plenty of places to get a cup of tea and a bite to eat, including G. Kelly Pie and Mash Shop, and E. Pellici cafe. At the east end of Bethnal Green Road you'll find the Museum of Childhood and Bethnal Green Gardens, both of which are worth a visit if you're in the area.

Getting a Stall
Contact the Tower Hamlets Central Market Office (see appendix) for a licence, then apply to:
Mansford One Stop Shop
152 Rushmead
Bethnal Green E2
071 739 8679

BROADWAY MARKET SW17

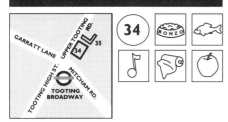

Upper Tooting Road.
Tube: Tooting Broadway (Northern Line).
Buses: 44, 57, 77, 127, 133, 155, 219, 264, 270 (Tooting Broadway).
Open: Monday-Saturday 9.30am-5pm.
Wednesday 9am-1pm.

One of the best things about this indoor market is the pet stall with its great display of tropical fish. If you prefer to eat our aquatic friends there's also a good fresh fish stall. Other attractions include a cheap stationers, a black music specialists, and D.N Fashion-selling cloth by the yard. The best fruit and veg is at the back entrance of the market- so be patient.

Getting a Stall
The stalls at Broadway Market are permanent lock-ups rented on a long term basis. If you're interested contact:
Mr Gerald Henderson
Market Manager
7 Longmead Road
Tooting
081 672 6613

TOOTING MARKET SW17

Upper Tooting Road
Open: Monday-Saturday 9.30am-5pm.
Wednesday 9am-1pm.

This indoor market is just a little further along Upper Tooting Road. It's a good place to get fruit and veg, fresh meat and fish, pet food, cheap shoes, baby wear, household goods and hardware. Most importantly, it has an unrivalled selection of

"Freedom for Tooting" T-shirts and badges, for those who still remember the expoits of Citizen Smith. Jackie Brafman owns a women's clothes stall in the market. Photos on every wall show Jackie with a host of show biz personalities and sports stars. The woman working there explains that he does a lot of work for charity, but doesn't like to talk about it. If all this star gazing makes you hungry there's The Grill and Sandwich Bar within the market, or Harrington's Pie and Mash Shop on Selkirk Road.

Getting a Stall
The stalls here are all permanent. If you're interested speak to someone at the tobacconist at the entrance to the market, from where the market is run.

BROADWAY MARKET E8

Broadway Market, between Westgate and Ada Street.
BR: London Fields (Liverpool Street).
Buses: 236 (Queensbridge Road). 30, 38, 277 (Graham Road).
Open: Friday-Saturday 9.30-4.30.

In the summer of '93 Hackney Council made a big effort to promote this small local market as a specialist flower market. The market blossomed in early spring with the local flower traders putting on a great show but, like French Marigolds, the bloom didn't last long. The market has now withered back to the few essential stalls selling fruit and veg, cut flowers and household goods. Perhaps Hackney Council will have another go this year...

Getting a Stall
Broadway market is run by Hackney Council (see appendix).

CHOUMBERT ROAD & RYE LANE MARKET SE15

Rye Lane, Peckham.
Peckham Rye BR (London Bridge, Holborn Viaduct).
Buses: 12, 37, 63, 78, 312, P3, P12 (Rye Lane).
Open: Monday-Friday 9am-5pm.

This is an unassuming, friendly market just off Rye Lane. It mainly specializes in fruit and veg, meat and fresh fish, although there are a few occasional clothes stalls to catch the eye. This is a great place to get Asian and Caribbean food, with lots of exotic fruit, vegetables, beans, meat and fish on offer. The refreshment available isn't quite so exotic, but the Choumert Cafe does a decent fry-up and a good cup of tea. Further along, north of the station, is Rye Lane Indoor Market. Here you can find fresh food, treats for your furry loved one, and a general junk stall selling anything from bikes to books.

Getting a Stall
The indoor market is run by Sherman & Waterman Associates ring 071 639 2463 or 071 732 8165 and ask for Mr Toomey.
For more information about Choumbert Road contact Southwark Council (see appendix).

CHURCH STREET NW8 & W2

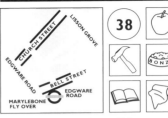

Church Street from Edgware Road to Lisson Grove.
Tube: Edgware Road (District, Metropolitan and Bakerloo).
Buses: 6, 16, 16A, 46, 98 (Edgware Road). 139 (Lisson Grove).
Open: Tuesday-Saturday 9am-5pm.

There has been a market on Church Street since the 1830's, although in those days it was called Portman market and only dealt in meat, fruit and veg. The present Church Street is a great deal more varied, selling anything from groceries to antiques. The western (Edgware Road) side of the market deals with the everyday necessities of life. From this part of the market you can get Nike and Champion T-Shirts for only £4.00, Bennetton duffle bags for £4.99, full-length denim or cotton dresses for between £15 and £20, as well as cheap bras for as little as £3. If you're one of those sad DIY characters, like myself, you'll be more excited by the hardware stall which sells five-piece metric spanner sets for only £2.75, and blow-lamps for £8.75, instead of £12.99. The food in this part of the market is also very good. Along with the usual fruit, veg and meat, you can find cheap eggs, dried fruit and nuts, confectionery including 3 bars of Swiss chocolate for £1, and if you want to treat that furry friend of yours there's a good pet food stall.

The eastern (Lisson Grove) part of the market has a very different atmosphere, reflecting this area's grander past before the railway separated it from Regents Park. Between Ashbridge and Plympton Street lies Alfies Antique Centre, with 4 floors of antiques and a roof top restaurant it's a great place to get lost in. This part of the street is full of surprises including the book stall selling a 1930's edition of "The Practice of Sex" for only £2, and good quality fabric for only £1 per yard. If you want to have a look for more bric-a-brac, Bell Street is just five minutes away walking south down Penfold Street.

If you're looking for refreshment there's the Regent Snack Bar on Edgware Road, which still has its original stainless steel and formica 1930's decor. There's also the famous Sea Shell on Lisson Grove, if you fancy traditional fish and chips .

BELL STREET NW1

Western end of Bell Street, between Edgware Road and Lisson Grove.
Open: Saturday 9am-5pm.

Bell Street is a great little market if you don't mind sifting through lots of clobber in search of something unusual. For those who like to see their prospective purchases clean, ordered and priced it is a place to avoid like the plague. On a recent visit it was possible to find a great cotton jacket for £1.50, and an excellent nylon 70's footballers top for only 50p. With nothing costing more than a couple of quid, you can afford to be a little reckless. Although the market isn't big there's enough here to keep you amused for half an hour, and there's always Church Street five minutes along Penfold Street if you long for the bustle of a larger market. If you're hungry after all that pottering try the Regent Snack Cafe on Edgware Road.

Getting a Stall
For details about Church and Bell Street contact Westminster City Council (see appendix)

CHRISP STREET E14

Market Square, Chrisp Street.
DLR: All Saints (Fenchurch).
Buses: 15, 40, 309, D8 (East India Dock Road).
Open: Monday-Saturday 9.30am-4pm.

With the completion of the new roof in December 1994, Chrisp Street appears to be doing quite well for itself. The market is at its best on a Friday or Saturday when you'll find a good range of fruit and veg stalls including more exotic things like jali, yams and cassava, simple fabrics for as little as £1 per yard, a shoe stall with canvas boots for only £5.99, cheap underware, quite a few stalls offering clothes and equipment for toddlers, a haberdashers, good value clothing and healthy looking bedding plants for only 80p per strip. Offering another sort of bedding, the linen stall had quite a few bargains, including 2 cotton pillow cases for £1. The shops and lock-ups in the square complement the market with a butchers and fishmongers. There are also several good places to get refreshment including J.P's Cafe, Chris's for traditional puddings and sausages, and George's Snack Bar which does a great cuppa and has outdoor seating.

Getting a Stall
You'll need to get a licence from Tower Hamlets Central Markets Office (see appendix) and then contact:
Chrisp Street Community Base
15 Market Square
Poplar E14 6AQ
071 537 2689

EARLHAM STREET MARKET WC2

Earlham Street.
Tube: Leicester Square (Northern and Piccadilly).
Buses: 14, 19, 24, 29, 38, 176 (Cambridge Circus).
Open: Monday-Saturday 9am-5pm.

In the days when Earlham Street was called Little Earl Street this was a thriving community market. The local community has long since made way for shops and offices, and the few stalls that remain depend upon passing trade. Although the bric-a-brac, clothing and book stalls are nothing special, the excellent fruit and veg and cut flowers stall still make this a market worth visiting if you're in the area .

Getting a Stall

Contact Camden Council for further details (see appendix).

EAST STREET SE17

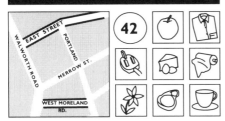

East Street between Walworth Road and Dawes Street.
Tube: Elephant & Castle (Northern, Bakerloo).
Buses: 12, 35, 40 45, 45A, 68, 171, 176, 184, P5 (Walworth Road).
Open: Tuesday-Saturday 8am-5pm. Thursday & Sunday 9am-3pm.

This vibrant south London market is at its biggest and best on Sundays, when both the shops and stalls are open for business. Here you can find simple women's clothes at good prices, many excellent haberdashery stalls, new electrical goods, good value nylon rucksacks and a limited range of fruit and veg. On a typical Sunday afternoon 15 oranges were £1, as were 2lb of lychees. At the Walworth Road end of the market is a provisions lock-up with quality cheese and chilled meats, although they don't offer anything too exotic. You can also find some excellent cloth for as little as £2 per yard, with off cuts for even less. On Sundays Blackwood Street, half way along, plays its part in maintaining the ozone layer; selling cheap plants at knock down prices, with fairly healthy looking fig and clematis plants for only £2 each. One surprise was the stall holder specializing in honey and candles produced by his own bee hives. He even had a photo of himself with his furry winged little chums to prove it! Another interesting stall offers rock salt cream and crystals for those shoppers with sore feet having walked the length of East Street. The stall has been there for years so there must be something to be said for it.

East Street has some good cafes for a cuppa and traditional high cholesterol breakfast. two of the best are Roffo's Sandwich Bar and Marie's Snack Bar, both on the right as you walk from Walworth Road. In the summer Roffo's Ice Cream Bar on the corner of East Street and Walworth Road is a great first stop before embarking on your quest for bargains.

WESTMORELAND ROAD SE17

Further south along Walworth Road
Open: Tuesday-Saturday 9am-4pm. Thursday 9am-1pm.
Sunday 8.30am-12.30pm.

During the week Westmoreland Road is a small local market with just a handful of stalls offering fruit and veg, household goods and on Saturdays the occasional clothes stall. On Sunday mornings the atmosphere is entirely different, with about fifty stalls offering bric-a-brac, furniture, cheap tools as well as old clothes, books and records. For those who love searching through clobber for something precious, this is paradise. Arment's Pie and Eel shop is a must if you're feeling peckish.

Getting a Stall

For more details about a stall at East Street or Westmoreland Road market contact Southwark Council (see appendix).

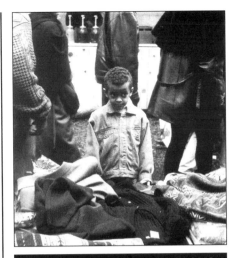

EXMOUTH MARKET EC1

Exmouth Market on the junction of Farringdon Road and Rosebery Avenue.
Tube: Farringdon (Circle, Metropolitan).
Buses: 19, 38, 171, 172 (Rosebery Ave)
63,168A, 259 (Farringdon Road)
Open: Monday-Saturday 9.30-4.30

Exmouth Market is not the hive of activity it once was, when Clerkenwell was a centre for Italian and Irish immigrants. It's now a quiet backwater, with only limited access to traffic. The best and most regular stall on the market is run by Jiri, who is there rain or shine until about 7.00pm. Among his assortment of books, clothes and bric-a-brac you can usually find something interesting. Al's Diner looks out onto the market and is a great place to get a cappuccino and watch the world go by.

Getting a Stall

For more details contact Islington Council (see appendix).

HAMMERSMITH MARKET W6

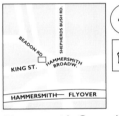

Hammersmith Grove, between King Street and Beadon Road.
Tube: Hammersmith (Metropolitan, Piccadilly and District lines).
Buses: 9, 10, 11, 33, 266, 267, 290, 391, H91, R69 (Hammersmith Broadway).
Open: Monday-Saturday 9am-5pm. Thursday 9am-1pm

In the last 25 years this market has been forced to move site three times to make way for development. The stall holders have shown admirable British pluck and now seem well established in Hammersmith Grove. Among the 10 or so regular stalls you can find good quality fruit and veg and great fresh fish at Fred Tydeman's stall. If you're looking for a good range of cheese don't forget The Big Cheese just round the corner on Beadon Road.

Getting a Stall

For more details contact Hammersmith and Fulham Council (see appendix).

HOXTON MARKET N1

Hoxton Street (Between Nuttall and Falkirk Street).
Tube: Old Street (Northern Line).
Buses: 22A, 22B, 48, 149, 55, 505 (central) 67, 243 (local).
Open: Monday-Saturday 9am-5pm.

During the week Hoxton Street is a quiet place with only a handful of stalls selling fruit and veg. On Saturdays the market gets into full swing with about 40 stalls offering new clothing, household goods and basic food stuffs. On the corner of Nuttall Street there's a good junk stall offering an assortment of clothes, books and furniture. The Wrong Rong cafe on Hoxton Square does a great cappucino.

Getting a Stall

For details contact Hackney Council (see appendix).

INVERNESS STREET NW1

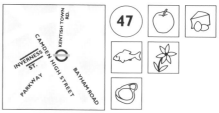

off Camden High Street
Tube: Camden Town
Buses: 24, 27, 29, 31, 68, 134, 135, 168, 214, 253 274, C2 (Camden High Street).
Open: Monday-Saturday 9am-5pm.
Thursday 9am-1pm.

Inverness Street Market is one of the best value little markets in London. Although there's only a small number of stalls, there's enough variety to buy all the groceries you need. Most of the stalls deal in fruit and veg. On a typical day you can find Galia Melons at 60p lb, bananas at 40p lb, 10 Kiwi fruit for £1.00 and cherries at 80p lb. The cheese stall is there from Wednesday to Saturday, offering a wide range of continental and British cheeses at below deli prices. From Thursday to Saturday the fish stall offers good value with Trout at £1.65 lb and Plaice at £2.49 lb. There are also fresh flowers on offer, a butchers and a stall specializing in eggs (half a doz. for 75p). If you're in the area and fancy a change from the hustle and bustle of trendies looking for clothes, it's well worth taking time out to visit.

Getting a Stall
For further details contact Camden Council (see appendix).

KILBURN MARKET NW6

Kilburn High Road opposite Birchington Road.
Tube: Kilburn Park (Bakerloo).
Buses: 16, 16A, 28, 31, 32, 206 (Kilburn High Road).
Open: Thursday-Saturday 9am-5pm.

Within the iron gates of this modern complex of lock-ups you can find the usual selection of fresh meat, fruit and veg, cut flowers, bags and toiletries. What makes the market worth a special visit is the pitch selling good quality trendy clothing, the cheap trainers stall, and Dave's Linens which offers king size duvets for only £10. Paul's Aquatic World isn't quite as exciting as it sounds, but it's a good place to stock up on food for your scaly or fury friend.

Getting a Stall
The pitches here are permanent lock-ups. An average site will cost £112 for the three days. For more details contact Michael Falton of Gray Sim Holdings on 0494 871 277

KINGSLAND WASTE E8

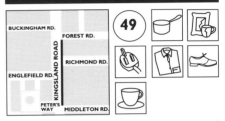

Kingsland Road between Forest and Middleton Road.
BR: Dalston Junction (Broad Street).
Buses: 22A, 22B, 67, 149, 243, 243A (Kingsland Road).
Open: Saturdays 9am-5pm.

On Saturdays the steady flow of pedestrians along Kingsland Road between Forest and Middleton Road changes into a mob gripped by consumer frenzy. Looking at some of the stalls it's hard to see what all the fuss is about. On offer are household goods (cheap detergent etc), fruit and veg (nothing too elaborate), new clothes, shoes of the cheap and tacky variety, several bric-a-brac stalls, and a few stalls selling second-hand electrical equipment (including a Nad amplifier for only £60). There were some genuine bargains to be had, including 4 chunky white mugs for £1.50. If you fancy something to eat there's Faulkner's Restaurant which does great fish and chips. Even on a good day this is nothing like Camden Passage - if you're looking for a gentile potter and charming cafes avoid this market at all cost.

Getting a Stall
For details contact Hackney council (see appendix).

LEWISHAM HIGH STREET SE13

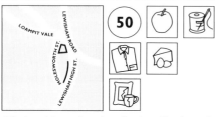

BR: Lewisham (London Bridge, Elephant & Castle) and Ladywell (Elephant & Castle).
Buses: 36, 75, 89, 108, 178, 181, 185, 199, 208, 225, 261, 284, 380, L1, P2, P4 (Lewisham High Street).
Open: General Market - Monday-Saturday 9am-5pm. Collectables Fair - Monday 10am-2pm.

Trapped between the traffic and the new shopping centre, Lewisham Market is not the thriving centre it was before the War. All that remains is a handful of stalls selling fruit and veg, eggs, haberdashery, cheap clothing, spectacles, and a few card and wrapping paper stalls at Christmas. On Mondays there's also a small bric-a-brac and collectables fair at Riverdale Hall off Rennell Street, around the corner from the market. Be sure to get there early as the stalls start packing-up at 2.00 rather than the 4.30 advertised.

Getting a Stall
The High Street market is run by Lewisham Council (see appendix). The Collectables Fair is privately run, contact John on 081 291 7493 for further details.

NAG'S HEAD MARKET N7

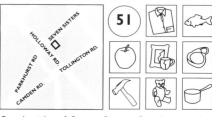

South side of Seven Sisters Road- near the junction of Holloway Road.
Tube: Holloway Road (Piccadilly).
Buses: 29, 43, 153, 253, 271, 279, X43 (Holloway Road).
Open: Monday-Saturday 9am-5pm. Sunday 9am-2pm.

This market used to be next to the eponymous Nag's Head pub on the corner of Holloway and Seven Sisters Road. The new purpose-built site doesn't have the chaotic atmosphere of the old market, but it's still a lively place, and the roof comes in useful on wet days. On Mondays, Tuesdays and Thursdays the market is a mixture of second-hand clothes and clobber, new household goods, toys, new clothing, tools, jewellery and a good assortment of food stalls offering fresh meat, fish and fruit and veg. On Wednesdays the market is entirely given over to second-hand bric-a-brac with lots of bargains on offer if you're prepared to join the throng and hunt for them. Fridays and Saturdays the market only has new things on offer, as well as the permanent food stalls. On Sundays the site becomes a flea market with a good range on offer for a Sunday potter. There are no groovy cafes in the area, and the roads in this part of town are a bit of a nightmare, but the place is still worth a visit. Bruno's Deli at 85, Parkhurst Road is a great little shop for anything Italian.

Getting a Stall
Bill Willingham is the manager of the market. He has an office on site if you want to visit in person, or give him a ring on 071 607 3527. The price of a stall varies from £8 on a Sunday to £40 on a Saturday.

NORTHCOTE ROAD SW11

West side of Northcote Road between Bennerley and Abyssinia Road.
BR: Clapham Junction (Victoria, Waterloo).
Buses: 115, 249, 319, G1 (Northcote Road). 35, 37, 49, 337 (Battersea Rise). 45A, 77, 77A (Lavender Hill).
Open: Monday-Saturday 9am-5pm.
Wednesday 9am-1pm.

This part of Battersea is definitely becoming more respectable. The market now has stalls selling exotic fruit and veg, and the selection at the fish stall borders on the adventurous. The permanent stall specializing in unicycles and juggling equipment adds to the impression that local residents may have more money than sense. On the opposite side of the road are a number of smart gift shops, Whittards for fine teas and coffees, and La Cuisiniere with everything for the kitchen. If you're in search of bargains there are a few good charity shops on the road. The Olympic Cafe is not as athletic as it sounds, but it does a good cup of tea if you need a rest from your exertions.

Getting a Stall
For details contact Wandsworth Council (see appendix.).

NORTH END ROAD SW6

East side of North End Road from Walham Grove to Lillie Road.
Tube: Fulham Broadway (District).
Buses: 28 (North End Road).
74, 190 (Lillie Road).
C4, 11, 14 , 391 (Fulham Broadway).
Open: Monday-Saturday 9am-5pm. Wednesday 9am-12.30pm.

This is a large and thriving market, particularly on Saturdays when it extends all the way from Walham Grove to Lillie Road. At the pot plant stall you could find a Bougainvillea for only £1.25, and a healthy Pepper Plant for £1.95. There are good value fruit and veg, cheese, egg and fish stalls. Among all this food can be found the occasional clothes, haberdashery and household goods stall - including one specializing in hoover parts. On the other side of the road (opposite Anselm Rd) an indoor market has started. If things take off this could be a welcome addition to the existing market. The best place to eat in the area is the Valley Lebanese Restaurant, which does anything from a cup of tea to a full-blown meal.

Getting a Stall
The small indoor market at 300 North End Road still has vacancies for as little as £10 per day. If you're interested either visit or ring them on 071 610 2667.
A stall at the outdoor market is more difficult to come by. Contact Hammersmith & Fulham Council for further details (see appendix).

QUEEN'S CRESCENT MARKET NW5

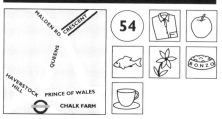

Queen's Crescent, between Malden and Grafton Road.
Tube: Chalk Farm or Kentish Town (Northern).
Buses: 24, 46 (Malden Road).
Open: Thursday 9am-1.30pm. Saturday 9am-5pm.

This is a small and friendly community market in the heart of Kentish Town. The range of goods on offer is nothing special. There are some good new clothes, fresh fruit, vegetables and fish, toiletries, pot plants and a very good stall selling food and toys for the furry friend in your life. At the crockery stall large, colourful cups are £1 each, and plates only 50p. The best thing about this market is the friendly atmosphere. Even on a Saturday people find time to stop for a natter. Among the good places to eat are The Market Cafe on Weedington Road, Bugsy Malone's and The Blue Sea Fish Bar.

Getting a Stall
For details contact Islington Council (see appendix).

QUEEN'S MARKET E13

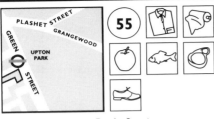

South of Upton Park Station, next to Queen's Road.
Tube: Upton Park (Metropolitan, District).
Buses: 238 (Plashet Grove). 58, 104, 162 (Green Street).
Open: Monday-Saturday 9am-5pm.
Wednesday 9am-12.30.

The addition of a roof to this market in 1979 has kept out the elements, but given the place a rather dark atmosphere. Despite this, on a Saturday there are over a hundred stalls offering cheap and cheerful clothes, Asian and African fabrics, a good selection of fruit and veg, fish, meat and a good value shoe stall. If you're in the area it's worth taking a look, you might find a bargain.

Getting a Stall
There's a waiting list of at least 18 months for a stall. For more details contact Waltham Forest council (see appendix).

RIDLEY ROAD E8

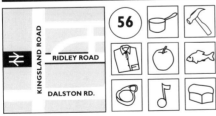

Ridley Road between Kingsland High Street and St Mark's Rise.
BR: Dalston Junction (Broad Street).
Buses: 22A, 22B, 67, 149, 243, 243A (Kingsland Road).
Open: Tuesday-Saturday 9am-5pm.

Ridley Road Market has been going since the 1880's. It's a lot bigger than it was then, and with the injection of Afro-Caribbeans, Asians and Turks to the community since the war, it's become a place where different races, cultures and foods come together. The mix is not always an easy one, but good humour and tolerance prevail. Fortunately the days when Mosely's Blackshirt's used to congregate on these streets are long gone.

The market has its fair share of good value hardware and household stalls. Among the bargains were four light bulbs for £1.00, and a four-way extension lead with 5 meters of flex for only £5.00. It also has a fair few stalls selling discontinued clothes, although the sizes available are usually limited. The market is best for food with an incredible range of fruit and veg, fish, meat and poultry. This is just about the only place in North London you can find live catfish for sale. Among the bargains you could get four Lemons for 25p, five Sweet Corn for £1.00, and Italian Grapes at 39p per lb. If you can't find what you're looking for the stall holders are very willing to give you advice on where you might get it. The meat is also good value with large chickens going for only £1.80, and there are all the things you might need for a caribbean dish from pigs snouts to dried fish.

On the southern side of the street are a great many shack style shops which spread out onto the street selling all sorts of food, as well as the occasional record shop playing reggae for all to hear. Probably the best shop on the street is the Turkish Food Centre (on the junction of Ridley Road and St Mark's Rise), where you can get Turkish Delight by the pound and fresh baked Turkish bread. If your needs are slightly less exotic there's always the Sainsbury's store on Kingsland High Street.

Getting a Stall
For details contact Hackney Council (see appendix).

LOCAL MARKETS

ROMAN ROAD E3

Roman Road from St Stephen's Road to Parnell Road.
Tube: Mile End (Central, Metropolitan and District)
Buses: 8 (Old Ford). 277, D6 (Mile End).
Open: Tuesday, Thursday and Saturday 8.30am-5.30pm.

Roman Road is one of the largest and longest established East End markets. One of its side streets is even called Beal Place, however the similarity with the TV EastEnders stops there. Roman Road is a lot cleaner and generally more pleasant than its fictional counterpart. That part of Roman Road leading to the market has fashionable clothes and record shops, a small photogallery, and a Buddhist centre with accompanying cafe. The area is also surprisingly green, with Victoria Park and the Grand and Hertford Union canals nearby.

The Market itself sells fruit and veg, linen and towels, fresh eggs, and has a vast selection of new clothing and shoe stalls. The clothing varies from mainstream youth clothing, to sensible floral designs for the over forties. Some of the best buys on a recent visit included high fashion (thick heel) sandals for £7.99, and ribbed T-shirts for as little as £4.99. The price and quality of the fruit and veg does vary, so have a look around before buying. There are also three indoor parts to the market although they don't contain very much of interest, with the exception of Dorothy Riley (spiritualist and healer), who offers private consultations for those eager to plan a future beyond the afternoon's grocery shopping.

If you're looking for culinary rather than spiritual sustenance, there are a great many cafes on Roman Road, the best being L. Randulfi who make great sandwiches and coffee, Ridley Bagel Bakery, and a traditional pie and eel shop. There are also a good many pubs in the area if you fancy a pint.

Getting a Stall

To trade at the outdoor market you'll need to get a licence from Tower Hamlets Central Markets Office (see appendix) and then contact:
Bow One Stop Shop
1 Ewart Place E3
081 980 1812
The indoor parts of the market are run by:
Sherman & Waterman Ass Ltd
568A Roman Road E3
081 981 0797 Mr Leslie.

SHEPHERD'S BUSH MARKET W12

Uxbridge Road.
Tube: Goldhawk Road or Shepherd's Bush (Metropolitan Line)
Buses 207, 607 (Uxbridge Road). 94, 237 (Goldhawk Road). 12, 49, 72, 105, 220 (Shepherd's Bush Green).
Open: Monday-Friday 9am-5pm. Thursday 9am-1pm.

Crammed into the narrow passageway parallel to the Metropolitan Line is a mixture of stalls, lock-ups and shops. On offer are African and Asian foods and clothes, fruit and veg, fabrics by the yard, things for the kitchen, a good range of bags, fresh fish, tacky jewellery and wigs. There's even a stall specializing in weight-training and martial arts equipment. If you're more interested in bric-a-brac don't forget about the Car Boot Sale next door, which is open Friday to Sunday (see section b. of the appendix for details). Refreshment can be found at the Arab food stall on the market. For tired feet and less adventurous taste buds try A. Cooke Pie & Eel shop or Cafe Rest, both situated east of the market on Goldhawk Road.

Getting a Stall
All the stalls are run on a long-term lease-hold basis. For more details contact:
Superintendents Office
Arch 174
Shepherds Bush Market
081 743 5089

SOUTHWARK PARK ROAD MARKET SE16

Market Place off Southwark Park Road.
BR: South Bermonsey (London Bridge).
Buses: 1, 199, 78 (Southwark Park Road).
P11, P13 (St James's Road).
Open: Monday-Saturday 9am-5pm.

Before the war this used to be one of the largest markets in South London with over 200 stalls on both sides of Southwark Park Road. In 1976 the local council succeeded where Mr Hitler failed, managing to move the market off the road and into the shopping precinct opposite Beatrice Road. The market is still going, with up to thirty stalls on a Saturday, selling plants, fresh fish, flowers, fruit and veg, as well as the occasional clothes stall.

Getting a Stall
The market is run by Southwark Council (see appendix).

LOCAL MARKETS

SWISS COTTAGE NW3

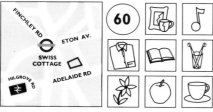

Winchester Road (behind the swimming pool).
Tube: Swiss Cottage (Jubilee)
Buses: 13, 31, 46, 82, 113, 268, C11, C12 (junction of Finchley and Adelaide Road).
Open: 9.30am-4.30pm all week (busiest on Saturdays).

Visiting Swiss Cottage Market in 1994, nearly 20 years since its idealistic beginnings, you'd be forgiven for thinking that both punk rock and Mrs Thatcher were nothing more than a bad trip. Although the market has been forced to move to its present site because of office development, it's still got a friendly community atmosphere, and some sense of its liberal, new-age ethos. The market is a mix of bric-a-brac, records and tapes, old and new clothes, paperback books, health foods, toiletries, videos, kids games, fruit & veg and pot plants. The style of stall varies from organized professionals to local amateurs. In general the standard of goods on offer and their display is very high, making the market a real potterer's paradise.

The community centre next door serves good hot and cold food and has open air seating adjacent to the market. Surrounding the market there's also a swimming pool, a small park and a great library with one of the largest philosophy & psychology sections in London. At the front of the library stands a bronze statue of Sigmund Freud by Oscar Nemon which is also worth a gander.

Getting a Stall
For more details contact the market manager on 071 722 4079.

TACHBROOK STREET SW1

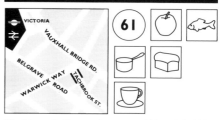

Tachbrook Street between Warwick Way and Churton Street.
Tube: Pimlico (Victoria). Victoria (Victoria, District, Circle).
Buses: 24 (Belgrave Road). 2, 36, 36B, 185, C10 (Vauxhall Bridge Road).
Open: Monday-Saturday 9.30am-4.30pm.

Tachbrook Street market is very small and not really worth exerting yourself to visit. It has a few good fruit and veg stalls, Wright's the fishmongers, and an assortment of stalls selling cards, household goods and shoes. The Pimlico area has a friendly atmosphere with lots of interesting and peculiar shops, and some excellent cafes and restaurants. Ivano's Italian grocers and Bonne Bouche bakery and patisserie are next door to each other on Tachbrook Street. Further along, on Upper Tachbrook Street, is Gastronomia Italia an appropriately named Italian deli and a few very interesting junk shops. Warwick Way - which transects upper Tachbrook and Tachbrook street - has an excellent Oxfam shop where you can find all sorts of bargains. If you're looking for something to eat, on Churton Street there's Chimes Wine and Coffee Bar, and Grumbles Restaurant if you want to stuff yourself. Churton Street also has a couple of interesting junk shops if you haven't yet had your fill of pottering.

Getting a Stall
Tachbrook Street is run by Westminster City Council (see appendix).

WALTHAMSTOW MARKET E17

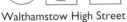

62 🍎 🍳 👔 👞

Walthamstow High Street
Tube/BR: Walthamstow Central (Victoria).
Bus: 20, 34, 48, 58, 69, 212, 215, 257, 275, W11, W15 (Walthamstow Central Station).
Open: Monday-Saturday 9am-5pm.

Although this is miles off the beaten track for most of you it's worth the trouble. Walthamstow can claim to be the longest street market in Britain, and anyone that manages to walk its length on a busy Saturday afternoon won't doubt it. The market sells nothing exceptional or out of the ordinary, but there are bargains to be found. Well made half-length leather jackets were only £85. Those with a more modest purse can find good quality leather belts for only £7.99. The market is very good for crockery, with large colourful mugs going for only 99p. There are also several haberdashers and stalls selling good quality fabric by the yard. Other things on offer include trendy boots and trainers, and more mundane necessities like pet food and kitchenware. If you need a rest and some refreshment there are lots of good places to eat. Rossi's of London is a classic cafe with wall to wall formica. There's also L. Manze Pie and Eel shop at no.76 which is worth a visit. The market's a real meeting place for the local community, and seems to thrive despite competition from the shops which line its route. With so many markets facing difficulties it's great to visit a market still in its prime.

Getting a Stall
For further details contact::
Trading Standards Office
8 Buxton Road
Walthamstow E17
081 520 4071

WELL STREET E9

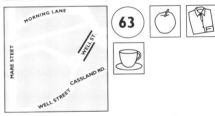

63 🍎 👔 ☕

Well Street - from Morning Lane to Valentine Road.
BR: Hackney Downs (Liverpool Street), Hackney Central (Broad Street).
Buses: 26, 30, 277 (Wick Road).
Open: Monday-Saturday 9.30am-4pm.

This market has a long history - Jack Cohen (the founder of Tesco) started trading here over 70 years ago. The place is now in decline with only a handful of stalls selling cheap clothing and groceries. Only the traditional pie and eel shop and the great bicycle repair shop make this a street worth going out of your way to visit.

Getting a Stall
For further details contact Hackney Council (see appendix).

North side of Whitechapel from Vallance Road to Brady Street.
Tube: Whitechapel (Metropolitan, District).
Buses: 25, 253 (Whitechapel Road).
Open: Monday-Saturday 8.30am-5.30pm.
Thursday 8.30am-1pm.

There's been a market on Whitechapel Road for centuries. The road is very wide to accommodate the hay market that stood here until the 1920's. Nowadays you can find an assortment of food, clothing, shoes, toiletries, towels and household goods. In the last 10 years the market has begun catering for the needs of the large Asian community living in the area. This makes it a great place to look for unusual Indian spices, pulses and vegetables with strange names like Begun, Valor and Maki. Whitechapel Road also has a store specializing in Indian groceries. The best place to go for a coffee and fry-up is Carlo's Cafe on Fulbourne Street. A little further down, at number 90, is the famous Blooms restaurant, a great place for artery clogging kosher treats. Don't forget the Whitechapel Gallery (just a few doors down from Blooms), if you get tired of the art it has a great coffee shop.

Getting a stall
Contact the Tower Hamlets Central Market Office (see appendix) for a licence, then apply to :
Collingwood One Stop Shop
4 Ashington House
Barnsley Street
E1 5RD
071 375 0951

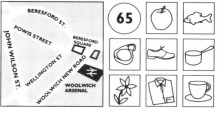

Beresford Square, Woolwich.
BR: Woolwich Arsenal (London Bridge).
Buses: 51, 96, 99, 122, 177, 178, 180, 244, 272, 380, 422, 469 (local). X53 (central).
Open: Tuesday-Saturday 8.30am-5pm.
Thursday 8.30am-1pm.

If you can be bothered to make the journey to Woolwich, the market is well worth a visit. About 40 stalls do business in view of the old Royal Arsenal. Here you can find fruit and veg, fresh fish and meat, cut flowers, great value bags, clothing, haberdashery, household goods, trainers and a stall specializing in football souvenirs. Many of the stall holders and quite a few of the customers have been coming here for generations, adding to the atmosphere of the place without making it hostile to strangers. For food try the Eel, Mash and Pie Cafe on Woolwich New Road.

PLUMSTEAD COVERED MARKET SE18

Plumstead Road (near Woolwich market).

This smaller indoor market offers army surplus goods, pet food and accessories, a small and rather limited sports stall, fabric by the yard, and a stall selling new age things like strange smoking devices and funny shaped candles. It's not worth going five minutes out of your way to visit, but it's only a stones throw from Woolwich market, so take a look.

Getting a Stall
Both markets are run by Greenwich Council (see appendix).

Wholesale Markets

INTRODUCTION

More than any other type of market in London the wholesale markets have undergone revolutionary change in the last 20 years. Borough and Smithfield are still on their old sites, but Covent Garden, Spitalfields and Billingsgate have all moved to larger industrial premises. Progress has meant increased profits for the more modern operations, but at a price not measured in monetary terms. The existing old markets are far more interesting, being more central with cafes and pubs open early to cater for the morning trade, and a generally more welcoming atmosphere.

The best thing about these markets is the people that do business from them; the anxious restaurateur searching for the best price, the market managers doing most of their trade over the mobile phone, and the porters having a chat and a joke when things are quiet. Although there are some bargains to be found they don't justify getting up at an unimaginable time in the morning and travelling miles to find them. The appeal of these markets is largely for those early birds who want to see London at work.

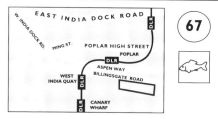

North quay of West India Dock, Isle of Dogs.
Docklands Light Railway: West India Quay.
Buses: 15, 15B, 40, D6, D8 (Poplar High Street).
Open: Tuesday-Saturday 5am-8.30am.

Billingsgate moved to this modern Docklands site in 1982, after trading near London Bridge for over 900 years. The old place had a great atmosphere and provided a contrast with the neighbouring City. The new concrete box looks inconspicuous surrounded by a motorway system and car park. The market is still an interesting place to visit with anything from a 40lb Pike to live lobsters on display. The porters no longer wear the famous leather basin hats used to balance baskets of fish, but they're still a friendly lot. If you want to find fishy bargains you'll be disappointed unless you're prepared to buy in bulk - although you could settle for a few packets of smoked Salmon at £1.50 each. Refreshment can be found at Crissy's Cafe which does a great mug of tea.

West side of Borough High Street.
Tube/BR: London Bridge (Northern and Network SouthEast).
Buses: N89, 17, 21, 22A, 35, 40, 43, 47, 48, 133, 344, 501, 505 (Borough High Street).
Open: Monday-Saturday 5.30am-10pm.

Borough market lays claim to being the oldest fruit and veg market in London, with antecedents dating back to medieval times. Although the market has moved about a bit since then, it's been at its present site since 1851. There's a great atmosphere about this cast-iron building sheltering in the gloom of overhead railway lines and exuding the sweet smell of cabbage.

Borough has resisted the trend to modernization, dealing with restaurants, grocers and small distributers rather than container business. The stall holders still make an effort to display their produce, giving passers-by something to look at rather than the lung full of diesal emission which is their only reward for visiting the larger fruit and veg operations. If you want to buy in smaller quantities BJD's stall will oblige, as will the Fruit & Cress Shop on Stoney Street which opens after 9am.

The Jubilee Cafe is at the back of the market. It's a great place to listen to punters and pitchers talk about business, both trying to fit as many expletives into a sentence as possible. The Wheatsheaf and Southwark Tavern on Stoney Street are open from 6am, as is the Globe on Bedale Street. On your way home take a peek at the now empty Hop Exchange a little further along the High Street. Another sign of this areas commercial past.

NEW COVENT GARDEN MARKET SW8

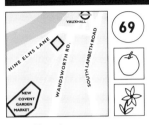

69

Nine Elms Lane.
Tube: Vauxhall (Victoria).
Buses: 2, 36, 36B, 44, 77, 77A, 88, 185, 322, 344 (Vauxhall Station).
Night Buses: N2, N36, N68, N70, N79, N87, N88 (Vauxhall Station).
Open: Monday-Friday 3.30am-10.30am.

If you're looking for a quaint traditional market populated with cheerful porters you'd better stick to Smithfields. New Covent Garden is big business. Since its move to Nine Elms from the West End in 1974 the place has thrived as the country's major distribution point for fruit, veg and flowers. The huge concrete complex with busy roads either side, and fork lift trucks zipping back and forth is not for the faint hearted. The fruit and veg part of the market isn't worth visiting unless you have a turnip fetish or enjoy watching lorries reversing. The place only caters for wholesale buyers and doesn't welcome the casual visitor looking for a couple of pounds of cheap spuds. The Flower Market is more interesting. Within its huge scented warehouse thousands of plants and cut flowers are on display. The best buys are the large terracotta pots for only £2.20 instead of £4 -£5. With plants and flowers you can save quite a bit, but only if you're prepared to buy in trays and boxes rather than single bunches. If a 50 stem bundle of tulips for £17 is a little beyond your means stick to flowers like Chrysanths or Anemone which can be bought in smaller quantities. There's a cafe overlooking the market if you fancy breakfast after your efforts.

SMITHFIELDS MARKET EC1

70

West Smithfields.
Tube: Farringdon, Barbican (Circle, Metropolitan, Hammersmith and City).
Buses: 8, 17, 22B, 25, 45, 46 171A, 221, 243, 259, 359, 501, 521 (Holborn Viaduct). 153, 279 (Smithfield). 55, 63, 505 (Clerkenwell Road).
Night Buses: N8, N76, N89, N95, N98 (St Paul's Station). N83 (Clerkenwell Road)
Open: Monday-Friday 5am-10.30 am.

If you can manage to leave a warm bed or nightclub sufficiently early, Smithfields meat market is a great place to visit. It's the last wholesale market in London to remain on its original site, resisting the trend towards automation and container storage, and still employing porters in white coats to carry the carcasses. This might not be the most efficient way of doing things, but it's a lot more fun to watch. The porters are a friendly lot, they joke amongst themselves and don't mind visitors taking photographs and having a look around, as long as you don't get in the way. The cast-iron building with its wide avenues and domed ceilings was designed by Horace Jones with the practical purpose of keeping the place well-aired and cool, but it's also wonderful to look at. Unless you have a very large carnivorous family, or a massive freezer you won't be able to buy from the various displays, but in the poultry section you can find smaller quantities of meat and poultry at about half the retail price. Vegetarians and those of a delicate disposition should be warned that there are a great many carcasses on display - including pink little piggies and furry (but very stiff) bunnies.

Lots of pubs and cafes open early to cater for the market. The Hope Pub on Cowcross Street does a great breakfast as does the Fox & Anchor on Charterhouse Street. The City Coffee House and Butts Snack Bar on St John Street are both good for a cuppa. If you're sick of meat after your visit to the market there's always Cranks on Cowcross Street.

Appendix

a. Getting a Stall

The markets of London offer a cheap way to trade without the overheads associated with a shop. More and more people are finding markets a good way to sell the goods that they have either bought or made. Stall holders vary from the professional, full-time company, employing people and turning over a considerable sum of money; to those who just go out once a week with a car load of second-hand goods to supplement their income.

Street trading is not something you can study at college, the best way to learn is by rolling up your sleeves and having a go. But don't think that just because practice makes perfect you don't have to plan things properly. Having browsed through the preceding pages and chosen the markets that you think will suit what you have to sell, visit them and see what they're like, and have a chat with some of the stall holders to see if they're doing well.

If you choose a private market you should be able to start without any problem, but they are more expensive. Council run markets are cheaper, but you need to get a casual licence from them and third party insurance before you can start trading. For further details about trading at a council market contact the relevant office, they all provide detailed information regarding rules and regulations, and may be able to offer advice about insurance. You can also get insurance with membership of The National Market Trader's Federation (address listed below) which costs £24 per annum. Once trading do your own marketing by keeping a track of what type of things you sell, and always calculate your net profit at the end of the day to see if all your efforts have paid-off. Lastly, always keep an eye out for ways to improve your stall and display things better. Sidney Street Shopfitting (address below) is a good place to go for display equipment, but you can find things second-hand or just thrown away on a skip that will serve a purpose.

Listed below are all the relevant council addresses if you're interested in trading at a council run market:

CAMDEN COUNCIL
Environmental Department
Consumer Protection Services Section
Camden Town Hall
Argyle Street
WC1H 8EQ
071 413 6917

GREENWICH COUNCIL
Consumer Protection and Environmental Health
Markets Department
Riverside House
Woolwich High Street
SE18 6DS
081 854 8888

HACKNEY COUNCIL
Environmental Services
Joseph Priestly House
49 Morning Lane
Hackney
E9 6ND
081 986 3123

HAMMERSMITH & FULHAM COUNCIL
Environmental Department
Consumer Services
Town Hall
King Street W6
081 748 3020 Mr John Pridham.

ISLINGTON COUNCIL
Cleansing and Transport Department
Albany Place
Benwell Road N7
071 477 4721

KENSINGTON & CHELSEA
This office deals with all sites along
Portobello Road and Golborne Road.
Market Office
72 Tavistock Road
London W11 1AN
071 727 7684

LEWISHAM COUNCIL
Street Trading Section
Laurence House
Catford Road SE6 4SW
081 695 6000

SOUTHWARK COUNCIL
Markets Section
Environment Services Department
151-153 Walworth Road
SE17 1RS
071 237 6677

TOWER HAMLETS
Each market in Tower Hamlets has a local
office called a One Stop Shop dealing with
its administration. Before approaching them
contact the central office to get a licence:
Central Market Office
The Brady Centre
Hanbury Street
London E1
071 247 3952

WALTHAM FOREST COUNCIL
Cliff Cole (Markets Officer)
Market Centre
Central Depot
Folkestone Road
London E6
081 472 1450 ext 26264

WANDSWORTH COUNCIL
Markets Department
Room 147
Town Hall
Wandsworth High Street
SW18 2PU
081 871 6384

WESTMINSTER CITY COUNCIL
Markets Department
City Hall
Victoria Street
Victoria SW1
071 828 8070 Mr Byron.

Listed below are other useful addresses for
insurance and display equipment:

THE NATIONAL MARKET TRADER'S FEDERATION
Hampton House
Hoyland
Barnsley
South Yorkshire
S7A 0HA
0226 749 021

SIDNEY STREET SHOPFITTINGS LTD
219-225 Commercial Road
London E1
071 790 0911

b. Car Boot Sales

Car Boot Sales are a welcome supplement to the established markets of London. The larger boot sales like Hackney Wick are massive, with hundreds of vehicles covering several square miles. Car boot sales began when landlords started using waste land and fields for occasional markets where people sold their junk from the boot of their car. Since those times things have really taken off with hundreds of car boot sales throughout the country, and many people making a living selling at them. Boot Sales are at their best when most of the traders are private individuals clearing out the house, rather than professionals trying to get rich quick. Many of the Boot sales now specify that no new goods can be sold in order to halt this trend.

Including boot sales within this publication is a bit of a risk as they change so quickly. To minimize this danger all the Boot Sales listed are long established, or run by established companies. Despite all the effort it's impossible to guarantee the longevity of a boot sale, so check before dragging yourself out of bed in search of bargains. It's worth looking through the local papers for adverts about forthcoming boot sales, particularly as schools and other needy institutions often run occasional events to raise money. Among the national papers The Sun is one of the worst for informed journalism, but the best for boot sale information, publishing a regular listing. Another good source of information is the bi-monthly publication, Car Boot Calendar which lists most of the major national boot sales and is available at any good newsagents.

Many of the boot sales listed are near to one of the markets mentioned within this book, when this is the case an (M) is placed next to the boot sales heading and the two are cross referenced. Weather you're trying to make a few quid or just looking for bargains, the boot sales of London are great places to visit, happy booting...

ACTON W3

Bromyard Leisure Centre, Bromyard Avenue.
Tube: East Acton (Central)
Buses: 105, 260, 283.
100 Pitches. Entry Fee £6 cars, vans (by arrangement only) £9.
Starts 9am every Sunday.
Phone Betty 0895 253 087 for further details.

BERMONDSEY SE1

Corner Tower Bridge Road and Bermonsey Street.
Tube: London Bridge (Northern).
Buses: 1, 42, 78, 188, 199, 701X.
70 Pitches. Entry Fee £6 cars, £8 vans.
Starts 6.30am sellers, 7am buyers, every Saturday.
Phone Danny Sherman 071 240 7405 for details.

BOUNDS GREEN N22

Bounds Green Junior School, Bounds Green Road.
Tube: Bounds Green
Bus: 84A, 102, 299, 221.
150 Pitches. Entry Fee £7 cars, £12 vans.
Starts 7am sellers, 8am buyers, every Sunday.
Phone Adrian Mildiner 081 889 9017 for details.

CHALK FARM NW1 (M)

The Old Bus Garage, Harmond Street, off Chalk Farm Road.
Tube: Camden Town (Northern Line).
Buses: C2, 27, 31, 274.
100 Pitches (undercover). Entry Fee £7 cars, £9 vans.
Starts 6.30am sellers, 7am buyers, every Saturday and Sunday
Phone Danny Sherman 071 240 7405 for details.

This undercover boot sale is just a few minutes north of Camden market (P.13-14), and worth a visit if only to escape the teenage hordes of Camden High Street.

CHELSEA SW10
Ashburnham Community Centre, Burnaby Street, Lots Road.
Tube: West Brompton (District).
Buses: 11, 19, 22, 45A, 49, 249, 319.
70 Pitches. Entry Fee £5 cars, £7 vans.
Starts 12.30pm sellers, 1pm buyers, every Saturday.
Phone 071 352 3335 for details.

CHINGFORD E4
Pickford's Cottage, Sewardstone Road.
BR: Ponder's End
Buses: 215, 333 (summer service).
200 Pitches. Entry fee cars and small vans £8, large vans £10.
Starts 7am, every Sunday.
Phone Andrew Roddick 081 529 3922 for details.

CROUCH END N8
Park Road.
BR: Hornsey. Tube: Highgate (Northern).
Buses: W3.
70 Pitches. Entry fee cars £7, Vans £11.
Starts 8am sellers, 9am buyers, every Saturday & Sunday.
Phone Fred Dobson 071 833 0780 for further details.

CRYSTAL PALACE SE19
(indoor) Jasper Road.
Buses: 2, 2A, 3, 63, 122, 137A, 157, 202, 249, 306, 322.
BR: Gipsy Hill, Crystal Palace.
45 Pitches. Entry fee £8.
Starts 8am sellers, 9am buyers, every Saturday & Sunday.
Phone Terry 081 761 3735 for details.

DOCKLANDS E16
Opposite City Airport, Royal Albert Dock.
Buses: 69, 276.
BR: Silvertown & City Airport.
200 Pitches. Entry Fee £5.
Starts 7am sellers, 8am buyers, every Sunday.
Phone Charfleet Promotions 071 474 3449 for details.

GREENWICH SE10 (M)
Unit 6, Thames Street.
Buses: 188 (Central), 199 (Local).
BR: Greenwich or Docklands Light Railway.
200 pitches. Entry Fee £5 cars, £15 vans.
Starts 7.30am buyers & sellers, every Sunday.
Phone Jackie 081 305 2167 for further details.
This flea market is on at the same time as the main market so it gets a mention in the review of Greenwich (P19).

GREENWICH SE10 (M)
Market Place, corner of Stockwell Street and Greenwich High Street.
(Transport details as above.)
100 pitches. Entry Fee £10.
Starts 7am sellers, 9am buyers, every Saturday.
Phone the Car Booter's Club 0905 610 800 for details.
This boot sale is really part of Greenwich market on Saturday. It occupies the area termed the Central Market (see P.19). It's much quieter on a Saturday, but there's still enough going on to make it worth visiting.

HACKNEY WICK
Hackney Wick Greyhound Stadium, Waterden Road, E15
BR: Hackney Wick.
Bus 6, 30, 236
500 Pitches, Entry Fee £10.
Starts 6am buyers and sellers, every Sunday.
Even on the coldest winter days this place is packed with bargain hunters. There's lots to see; new and used electrical equipment, clothes, household goods, toys, records... there is even a stall specializing in photocopiers! It's a very popular place so you'll have to be there by 6am to be sure of getting a stall.

HARROW HA3
Claremonnt High School, Claremont Avenue, Kenton.
Tube: Queensbury, Kingsbury (Jubilee).
Buses: 183, 114, H10, H18.

Pitches: 200.
Entry Fee: £5 cars, £8 vans.
Starts 7.30am sellers, 8.30am buyers, every
Saturday.
Phone Mrs Sims 081 204 4442 for details.

ISLINGTON N5
Highbury Roundhouse, 71 Ronalds Road.
Buses: 43, 279, X43, 30, 271 (central).
4, 277 (Local).
Tube & BR: Highbury & Islington.
60 Pitches (in and outdoors).
Entry Fee £6.
Starts 8am alternate Sundays.
Phone June or Sue 071 359 5916 for details.

ISLINGTON N1
Goswell Road (opposite Angel station).
Tube: Angel (Northern).
Buses: 4, 19 30, 38, 43, 56, 73, 153, 171A,
214, 279.
50 Pitches.
Entry Fee £6 cars, £8 vans.
Starts 6.30am sellers, 7am buyers, every
Saturday and Sunday.
Phone 071 240 7405 for details.

ISLINGTON N7
Holloway Road (opposite the Odeon cine-
ma).
Tube: Holloway Road (Piccadilly).
Buses: 43, 153, 271, 279.
100 Pitches.
Entry Fee £5 cars, £8-12 vans.
Starts 7.30am sellers, 8am buyers, every
Saturday.
Phone 0992 717 198 or 0850 668 077 for
details.

KENSAL GREEN
HELEN'S CAR BOOT SALE
Junction of Chamberlayne and Harvest
Road.
Tube: Kensal Green (Bakerloo).
Buses: 6, 52, 302.
100 Pitches.
Entry Fee £5 cars, £10 vans.
Starts 8.30am buyers, 9am sellers, every
Sunday.
Phone 081 960 6521 for details.

KILBURN NW6
Kilburn College, Carlton Vale.
Tube: Kilburn Park, Queens Park
(Bakerloo).
Buses: 6, 28, 31, 36, 46.
80 Pitches.
Entry Fee £7 cars, £10 vans.
Starts 8am buyers and sellers, every Sunday.
Phone 071 625 7730 for details.

LEWISHAM SE13
The Lewisham Centre Muti Storey Car
Park, Molesworth Street.
BR: Lewisham (London Bridge).
Buses: 36, 75, 89, 108, 178, 181, 185, 199,
208, 261, 284, P4.
200 Pitches.
Entry Fee £8.50 cars, £12.50 vans.
Starts 6.30am sellers, 7am buyers, every
Sunday.
Phone 0426 924 201 for details.

PORTOBELLO ROAD W11   (M)
Under the Westway canopy.
Tube: Ladbroke Gove (Hammersmith &
City), Notting Hill Gate (Central).
Buses: 7, 15, 23, 28, 31, 70.
200 Pitches.
Entry Fee £7 Cars and Vans.
Starts 7am sellers, 9am buyers, every
Sunday.
Phone Country Wide 071 221 4410 for
details.
If you want to know more about the atmos-
phere of the place on a Sunday see
Portobello Market (P.21-23).

APPENDIX

SHEPHERD'S BUSH W12   (M)
Steptoe's Yard, Goldhawk Road.
Tube: Goldhawk Road (Hammersmith & City).
Buses: 12, 49, 95, 105, 207, 237, 260, 607.
100 Pitches.
Entry Fee £8 cars, £10 vans.
Starts 6am sellers, 6am buyers, every Friday, Saturday and Sunday.
Phone Mr Caskie 071 602 2699 for details.
This boot sale runs parallel to Shepherd's Bush (see P.57).

SOUTHFIELDS SW19
Burghley Hall Pub, 33 Princes Way.
Tube: Southfields (District).
Buses: 14, 39, 85, 93.
60 Pitches.
Entry Fee cars and vans free.
Starts 7.30am sellers, 8am buyers, every Sunday.
Phone Donna Budd 081 788 5180 for details.

TOTTENHAM N15
Tottenham Community Sports Centre, Tottenham High Road.
Tube: Seven Sisters, Tottenham Hale (Victoria).
Buses: 149, 259, 279, 359.
68 Pitches.
Entry Fee £7 cars, £9 vans.
Starts 7am sellers, 7am buyers, every Thursday.
Phone Countryside Promotions 0992 468 619 for details.

WEST HAMPSTEAD NW6
Opposite West Hampstead tube station.
Tube/BR: West Hampstead (Jubilee, Network SouthEast).
Buses: 28, 139, C11.
70 Pitches.
Entry Fee £8 cars, £10 vans.
Starts 7am buyers and sellers, every Saturday and Sunday.
Phone Ron 0923 770 515 (pm) for details.

WHITECHAPEL E1   (M)
Behind The Blind Beggar Pub, Whitechapel Road.
Tube: Whitechapel (District, Hammersmith & City).
Buses: 5, 8, 15, 25, 40, 67, 253.
600 pitches.
Entry Fee £8 cars, £12 vans.
Starts 5.20am sellers, 6.20 buyers, every Saturday and Sunday.
Phone Danny Sherman 071 240 7405 for details.
This is a long established boot sale just five minutes walk from Brick Lane (P. 8-9). If you're in the area be sure to take a look.

WIMBLEDON SW19
Community Centre, Haydons Road.
Tube: Wimbledon (District).
Buses: 57,93, 131, 155, 156, 200.
60 Pitches.
Entry Fee £6 cars, £8 vans.
Starts 8am sellers, 9am buyers, every Thursday.
Phone 081 675 0673 for details.

WOOD GREEN N22
New River Sports Centre, White Hart Lane.
Tube: Wood Green (Piccadilly).
Buses: 67, 112, 123, 141, 230, 243, W4.
65 Pitches.
Entry Fee £7 cars, £9 vans.
Starts 7.30am buyers and sellers, every Friday.
Phone Countryside Promotions 0992 468 619 for details.

If you're interested in trading at a boot sale and want a few ideas the only publication on the subject is Roger Morgan's optimistically entitled, £500 a Week from Car Boot Sales (Imperia Books) £6.99 (ISBN 1-897656-03-3).

GENERAL INDEX

INDEX

75

	M	T	W	T	F	S	S
1. Brick Lane							●
2. Brixton Market	●	●	▲	●	●	●	
3. Camden Market				▼	▼	●	●
4. Covent Garden	a	●	●	●	●	●	●
5. Greenwich Market						●	●
6. Portobello Road Market	▼	▼	▼	▼	▼	●	
7. Petticoat Lane Market	▼	▼	▼	▼	▼		●
8. Bayswater Road & Piccadilly Market							●
9. Bermondsey (New Caledonian) Market					●		
10. Camden Passage			●	b		●	
11. Charing Cross Collector's Fair						●	
12. Farringdon Road Market	●	●	●	●	●		
13. Hampstead Community Market						●	
14. Merton Abbey Mills Market						●	●
15. Piccadilly Market					●	●	
16. Platts Market						●	
17. The Courtyard Market	●	●	●	●	●	●	
18. Berwick Street Market	●	●	●	●	●	●	
19. Chapel Market		●	●	▲	●	●	▲
20. Columbia Road Market							●
21. Spitalfields Market							●
22. Charlton Street Market	▲	▲	▲	▲	▲		
23. Leadenhall Market	●	●	●	●	●		
24. Leather Lane Market	▲	▲	▲	▲	▲		
25. Lower Marsh Street	▲	▲	▲	▲	▲	▲	
26. Strutton Ground Market	▲	▲	▲	▲	▲		
27. Whitecross Street Market	▲	▲	▲	▲	▲		
28. Earl's Court Sunday Market							●
29. Nine Elms Sunday Market							●
30. Wembley Sunday Market							●
31. Balham Market	●	●	●	▲	●	●	
32. Battersea High Street Market	●	●	●	●	●	●	
33. Bethnal Green Road Market	●	●	●	▲	●	●	
34. Broadway Market (SW17)	●	●	▲	●	●	●	
35. Tooting Market	●	●	▲	●	●	●	
36. Broadway Market	●	●	●	●	●	●	
37. Choumbert Road & Rye Lane Market	●	●	●	●	●		
38. Church Street Market		●	●	●	●	●	
39. Bell Street Market						●	

	M	T	W	T	F	S	S
40. Chrisp Street Market	●	●	●	●	●	●	
41. Earlham Street Market	●	●	●	●	●	●	
42. East Street Market		●	●	▲	●	●	▲
43. Westmoreland Road Market		●	●	▲	●	●	▲
44. Exmouth Market	●	●	●	●	●	●	
45. Hammersmith Market	●	●	●	▲	●		●
46. Hoxton Market	●	●	●	●	●	●	
47. Inverness Street Market	●	●	●	▲	●	●	
48. Kilburn Market				●	●	●	
49. Kingsland Waste Market						●	
50. Lewisham High Street Market	●	●	●	●	●	●	
51. Nag's Head Market	●	●	c	●	●	●	●
52. Northcote Road Market	●	●	▲	●	●	●	
53. North End Road Market	●	●	▲	●	●	●	
54. Queen's Crescent Market				▲		●	
55. Queen's Market	●	●	▲	●	●	●	
56. Ridley Road Market		●	●	●	●	●	
57. Roman Road Market		●		●		●	
58. Shepherd's Bush Market	●	●	●	▲	●		
59. Southwark Park Road Market	●	●	●	●	●	●	
60. Swiss Cottage Market	●	●	●	●	●	●	●
61. Tachbrook Street Market	●	●	●	●	●	●	
62. Walthamstow Market	●	●	●	●	●	●	
63. Well Street Market	●	●	●	●	●	●	
64. Whitechapel Market	●	●	●	▲	●	●	
65. Woolwich Market		●	●	▲	●	●	
66. Plumstead Covered Market		●	●	▲	●	●	
67. Billingsgate Market		★	★	★	★	★	
68. Borough Market	★	★	★	★	★	★	
69. New Covent Garden Market	★	★	★	★	★		
70. Smithfield Market	★	★	★	★	★		

KEY:

Open all day	●
Half day opening	▲
Market partially open	▼
Only open early mornings	★
Antiques market (see P.16-17)	a
Book Market (see P.29-30)	b
Bric-a-brac market (see P.52)	c

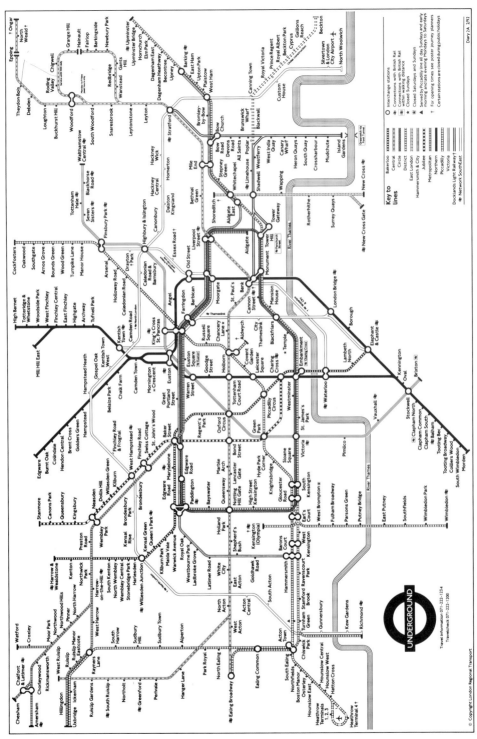

UNDERGROUND

Travel information 071-222-1234
Travelcheck 071-222-1200

© Copyright London Regional Transport

Key to lines

Bakerloo	
Central	
Circle	
District	
East London	
Hammersmith & City	
Jubilee	
Metropolitan	
Northern	
Piccadilly	
Victoria	
Docklands Light Railways	
Network SouthEast	

○ Interchange stations
⊖ Connections with British Rail
⊛ Connections with British Rail within walking distance
★ Closed Saturdays and Sundays
● Closed Sundays
▲ Served by Piccadilly line all day Sundays and early morning and late evening Mondays to Saturdays
✈ For opening times see poster journey planners
‡ Certain stations are closed during public holidays

Diary 2A 2/92

LRT Registered User No. 94/2006

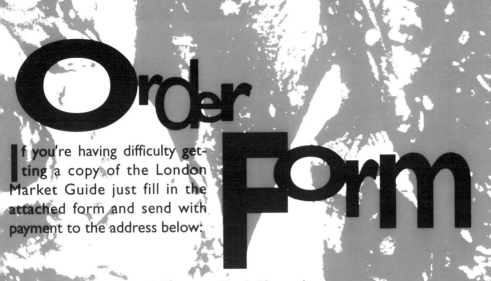

Order Form

If you're having difficulty getting a copy of the London Market Guide just fill in the attached form and send with payment to the address below.

**Metro Publications
PO Box 6336
London
N1 6PY**

We'll send you as many copies as you like without charging for postage, but please allow 2 weeks for delivery.

✂ -

Please send me
copy/copies of
The London Market Guide

1	2	3
☐	☐	☐

I enclose payment of
(cheques made payable
to Metro Publications)

£3.99	£7.98	£11.97
☐	☐	☐

Name: _____

Address: _____

_____

Please keep me informed
about forthcoming publications

_____

☐

_____